THE CANKLOW MURDER

Margaret Drinkall

Chris Drinkall

Contents

Chapter One: John and David Coe 3
Chapter Two: The Murder 8
Chapter Three: The Inquest 14
Chapter Four: John Henry Wood..20
Chapter Five: The Capture of Wood and the Second Inquest ...31
Chapter Six: Magistrates Court Appearances............................38
Chapter Seven: Magistrates Court. The Second Day. 46
Chapter Eight: The Trial and the Prosecutions Case. 54
Chapter Nine: The Defence and the Judges Summing Up. 59
Chapter Ten: The Condemned Man 67
Chapter Eleven: Conclusions..74
Other Books By Margaret Drinkall 78

Chapter One: John and David Coe

The village of Canklow is situated about a mile outside of the town of Rotherham which in the 1880's was described as a rural area consisting of fields, woods and grazing lands. Few houses existed, although there were some outstanding buildings to be seen from Canklow Road. The oldest was a corn mill owned by the Duke of Norfolk, which over the years had been leased to various tenants. Another was a brewery owned by R J Bentley, which had opened in 1840 and employed several local men. Also visible was Canklow House or Hall containing spacious outbuildings, gardens, stables and pleasure grounds. However for the people of Rotherham the biggest attraction to the area is Canklow Wood, which is a famous beauty spot of the period, once again owned by the Duke of Norfolk. There, many of the townsfolk would walk and have picnics on lands which had been inhabited since the days of the Romans. For many years Earl Fitzwilliam's foxhounds would meet regularly at Canklow Wood or outside the mill itself. There the hounds would pursue the fox over the fields and hedges of the four adjoining villages of Canklow, Brinsworth, Wickersley and Whiston.

In February of 1880 John Coe was a young man aged 26, a farm labourer living with his parents, John and Mary Coe at Brinsworth. He was said to have been a respectable, hard working young man by all who knew him, who possessed a general good character and steady habits. Coe was described as being very likeable with a sense of humour, as well as possessing a good singing voice. When not working, he tended to frequent the Dusty Miller Inn on Westgate, where he would entertain locals with his singing. It was said that:

'his presence there was always accompanied by a good deal of merriment, as he would for hours altogether, entertain the company with a copious selection of ditties, which were always well received'.

John had been employed by Mr George Thompson of Howarth Grange, Brinsworth, but when his employer decided to move to

Warwick John found himself out of a job. Even though he was not working he was known to be a very generous man, who often helped out his uncle David Coe aged 44 years with loans of money. David was not married and until the previous Christmas had been employed by Mr Brightmore another farmer of Brinsworth. At that time he had been living with his brother-in-law Thomas Cliffe at Brinsworth, who having lost a hand managed with a hook. David was not an unkind man, but was known to be subject to mood swings due to depression, and it was said that at such times he would not speak to anyone for a couple of days. Nevertheless he seemed fond of his nephew John and they were often seen out and about together, particularly following the Fitzwilliam hounds. However David had developed a taste for alcohol, and a year previous to the murder had been brought before the magistrates charged with drunkenness. This was most unusual as David Coe was reported to be a peaceable man, who was not to be quarrelsome even 'in his cups'. By 1879 it was said that he and his nephew had been on very good terms as they had a lot in common, both being pigeon fanciers who occasionally swapped birds.

On 18 February 1880 John and David Coe had spent the day following the Fitzwilliam hounds, who on this occasion had met at Wickersley Bar. In those days, no one saw anything cruel about foxhunting and hundreds of local people would eagerly follow the hounds as they chased down their quarry. As a pastime it was very popular and the exploits of the hounds were regularly reported in local newspapers. In December 1876 the *Sheffield and Rotherham Independent* proudly reported the poor animal's last frantic journey in its attempt to escape its pursuers. In horrific detail the reporter stated that the fox:

'crossed the Rother Valley for Canklow Wood. Driven thence he ran through the Boston Castle grounds and got into a drain on the left side of the Canklow Road, opposite Mr Bentley's Brewery. Very quickly however he was forced from his hiding place and gave up his brush to be added to the trophies of the season and his body to satisfy the instinctive craving of his eager pursuers'.

Despite this many local men saw the foxhunt as a pleasant day out and John and David Coe were no exception. After the hunt had finished the two men went to the Masons Arms at Wickersley, and subsequently had a merry time together. John was asked for a song or two, to which he willingly obliged. At 4 pm the couple were at the Chequers Inn at Whiston where they both remained drinking until about 8 pm. The landlord Mr Robert Elliott later stated that both John and David were not intoxicated, but had enjoyed themselves 'in a quiet orderly fashion'. The two men were joined, just after 6 pm by John Henry Wood aged 27. Unlike the other two men, he was well known to the Rotherham authorities, having only been released from prison three months previously. However Wood was not well known to John and David Coe, although they readily invited him to come and have a drink with them. At the time there was a man named Edward Wilkinson in the Chequers Inn, who had also had been following the Fitzwilliam hounds. He had in his possession a fine, thin stick which he told John he had cut from a hedge and peeled only that day. John Coe possessed a green holly stick, and for a while the two men were busy engaged in pointing out the merits of their own sticks, which eventually they agreed to exchange. The landlord stated that prior to his departure, John Coe had changed a half sovereign, which was worth about 10s (50p). At the time the two men left, John would still have had nine shillings in silver and copper in his pocket (the equivalent of around £58 in 1880). He also had a silver Geneva watch on his person which he had consulted throughout the afternoon. As the three men left the Chequers, the two Coe's were heading towards Rotherham, Wood said that he would accompany them (even though he lived at Whiston). The three men were then seen heading towards the town.

A statement made later by David Coe related that the men went past Oakwood and were walking down Moorgate when, because of the amount of alcohol he had consumed, David fell behind. He also told the police that he could barely remember anything of the walk home, and very little after leaving the Chequers Inn. David said that Wood and his nephew left him at Moorgate after he had fallen down several times into the road and hurt his arm. When the two men left him he went to his aunts house, Betsy Roddis, a widow who lived on Clough Road, Masbrough Common. David arrived there about midnight, but when she saw the state of him Mrs Roddis accused him of being 'in a beastly state of drunkenness', nevertheless she allowed him to spend the night on her sofa. The following morning about 5 am David left, although his aunt tried to get him to have some breakfast with them, but he refused. He went to the Masbrough Forge where he saw 'a chap or two about some business'. Public houses in Rotherham opened early in the morning at the time and about 5.30 am David went firstly to the Three Horse Shoes on Westgate where he called for a pint of beer. The landlord, Benjamin Smith served him and as there were no other customers, the two men fell into conversation together. David stated that he and his nephew had followed the hunt the previous day as far as Roche Abbey. At that point another customer entered the house and the landlord went to serve him.

David's later statement to police officers continued, saying that he then went to the White Swan and asked the landlord, Mr Lister for a pint of beer. The landlord later confirmed that David had drunk it quietly in one of the rooms, where he remained until 8.45 am. Then he had another pint of beer before leaving there shortly before 9 am and heading towards Brinsworth. David told officers that he was due to meet up with his nephew, as agreed the previous day, in order to exchange some pigeons. He stated that as he approached Canklow, he had noticed some police officers in a field and walking around a stack of hay. On the footpath in front of him was a man and a woman and David casually asked them 'what's amiss'. They told him 'its a man that's gotten killed'. He thought no more about it at the time, before he calling in at the house of a Mrs Brightmore at Brinsworth, who gave him a shilling for some work he had previously done for her. On being paid, David immediately bought himself another pint at a local beer house before heading towards John Coe's parents house. Before he reached it however, a police officer, Sergeant Morley saw him and told him 'you're the man that's wanted'. Bewildered he asked the officer what he was wanted for, but the man just told him 'your going to have to come with me'.

Reports that the uncle of the deceased man had been arrested for the crime of murder was swiftly printed in most of the local and national newspapers, as was the condition of the chief suspect. Despite the assertion made by the landlord of the White Swan that David had drunk his beer quietly and peaceably, by this time he was reported as being too drunk to speak. As a consequence it was decided not to bring him before the magistrates that morning, until he had quite sobered up. He was brought back along Canklow Road in a cab and seeing David Coe with Sergeant Morley the crowd at Canklow drew their own conclusions. Anxious spectators ran into the road and followed the cab back into Rotherham. It was noted by those who caught sight of the prisoner that he had an almost stupefied look on his face, and that he clearly had no idea of what was happening to him.

Chapter Two: The Murder

On the morning of Thursday 19 February 1880 before the murder had been reported, the shopkeepers and businessmen of Rotherham were preparing for the duties of the day. As the morning went on however, rumours were heard to circulate the town that a body had been found at Canklow. A man had been seen by several witnesses lying in a field at the side of a haystack although none of them, for one reason or another, chose to investigate further. It seems that one of the first, a man called George Hall was passing Canklow Road seated on his wagon around 7 am. He saw a man lying with his back against a stack of hay and noted red marks around his head, however he was not close enough to see clearly, although he thought he saw one of his legs move. Having assumed that the man had put a red handkerchief over his head to protect it from the rain, which had fallen at intervals that morning, he continued on his journey. The position of the murder was described by the *Sheffield and Rotherham Independent*, dated 20 February as taking place:

'A short distance on the Canklow Road, not far from Bentley's Brewery on the left hand side, is a roadway leading to fields on the hill side, known as Hattersley Well Lane. The road runs up to land just under the shadow of Boston Park. About fifty yards up the lane in a field tenanted by Mr John Jarvis is a large straw stack'.

About 7.30 am a man delivering milk called Samuel Bendin of Brinsworth was going along Canklow Road towards Rotherham with his horse and cart, when he too noticed the body of a man reclining against a stack of hay. Bendin was in a rush to complete his deliveries, and he also assumed that it was a man sleeping off the excesses of the previous night. At some time around 8 am a man called Joseph Hawksworth, a moulder of Catcliffe, was on his way to work at Owen's Foundry on Westgate, when he too passed the field and saw the man's body. However, unlike the previous witnesses, he noticed something strange about the position in which the body was lying. He stopped and was still observing the body when he was overtaken by two other men from Catcliffe, John and George Swallow who were father and son. Hawksworth pointed out the body and finally, with some trepidation, the three men approached the figure. They were horrified to see that the man was surrounded by a pool of blood and, rather than a red handkerchief on his head, his forehead and face had been smashed in. So badly injured was the man that none of the men recognised him, although they noted that he was dressed in labourer's clothing. This consisted of a coat, a black vest, corduroy trousers and a red neckerchief worn around the neck. Crucially, it was noted by the men that blood was still oozing from the man's wounds, indicating that some life still remained in the body. The men also noted that two sticks were found nearby, one, which looked like the murder weapon, was a heavy hedgestake broken in two. The other was a light stick which had recently been cut from a hedge and freshly peeled.

George Swallow quickly ran into Rotherham to fetch the police, whilst the other two men remained with the body. The area was so isolated that the only houses that could be seen were 400 or 500 yards away. Nevertheless the news of the murder had spread so quickly around the area, that even though two officers, Police Constable Ellis and Sergeant Thomas Morley had been quickly despatched, by the time they arrived they found about twenty other people crowding around the body. They also noted that there was also a steady stream of people heading from the town towards the site of the murder, all anxious to see the spot where a man had been killed. The two officers arrived about 8.55 am and they found that the body was still warm. Straw had been pulled from the stack as if to make up a bed to lie on. Walking around the stack the Sergeant found the hedgestake, which he described as being about a yard and a half long and at least two inches thick in circumference. There could be little doubt that this was the weapon that had been used to kill the man, in a manner so frenzied that blood was spattered to a good height up the stack. It was reported that the crowd swiftly became so large that the two officers had the most difficulty in restraining them, urging the people to keep back at all costs.

At 9.30 am the landlord of the Prince of Wales Feathers public house on Westgate, Mr William Gabbitas appeared, and Sergeant Morley requisitioned his services in order to keep back the ever growing crowd. By this time PC Ellis had been sent to fetch Dr

Junius Hardwicke the Medical Officer of the workhouse on nearby Alma Road. He arrived just shortly after 9.25 am and quickly noted the murdered man's disfigured features. He also saw that his skull had been so damaged that at the frontal bone, part of the brains were protruding. The surgeon immediately ordered that the body be removed to the dead house at the workhouse. A light cart belonging to John Mellor of Rotherham was commandeered for the task, and the body was lifted onto the cart and taken away. By this time the Superintendent of Police, Mr Gillett arrived on the scene, to take charge of the case. When he heard that the body had been removed, he went to the workhouse and requested Dr Hardwicke to keep out all observers, until a post mortem could be carried out. The Surgeon agreed and locking the door of the dead house put the key in his pocket. Mr Gillett then returned back to the murder site. Sergeant Morley told the Superintendent that in order to identify the body, he had searched the dead man's pockets but found nothing, as his pockets were empty.

The face of the dead man had been washed at the workhouse and had been identified as that of John Coe of Brinsworth. Police enquiries quickly established that he had been drinking the night before with his uncle David Coe, who immediately became a suspect. It quickly became known that David had been seen earlier that day heading along Canklow Road towards Brinsworth. Upon being given this information, Sergeant Morley chartered a cab and went to Brinsworth where he found David in the street. The sergeant asked David to come with him, but found he was so drunk he could barely speak. Nevertheless the man was informed that he was being arrested on suspicion of the murder of his nephew John Coe, to which news David appeared somewhat stunned. The prisoner was then taken to the police station and charged with the murder of his nephew to which he made a rambling reply. He said:

'I have never seen him since I left him at Whiston last night. I am certain I have never done nowt of this in my life before and I am sorry I am in for a job of this sort. I am certain I never did nowt amiss to him. I saw him at Wickersley yesterday when we were hunting together. I should be a soft head to do owt to him I wish he wor in heaven. I'll tell you what he did to me yesterday: he gave

me a shilling for some beer. That's the worst he said to me. I am as innocent as you are at this present moment'.

At the station he was examined and minute stains of blood were found on his left hand, his clothes and chaff from hay on his boots. When asked about the blood David claimed that the blood was from a cockerel he had killed a few days previously. David Coe was then taken to the cells where he was left overnight. Dr Cobban, the Medical Officer of Health who was in the police office, was asked to examine David's clothing which he did. He confirmed that he had found some bloodstains and gave his opinion that they could be human blood.

The following morning David Coe was sober enough to make a proper statement regarding his whereabouts on the night of the murder, and the following morning. Shortly afterwards he was brought before the magistrates and the Mayor of Rotherham, Alderman Harrison at the police court. At an early hour crowds gathered outside the court house anxious to catch sight of the prisoner. When the Mayor arrived about 10.45 am the crowd surged forward, but they were disappointed. Several burly officers had been positioned at the door ensuring that the crowd was unable to see the prisoner. The door of the court house were closed firmly until David Coe was brought into the courtroom and placed in the dock, and only then were the public admitted. The prisoner was described as being:

'A man of medium height dressed in a light smock, generally worn by farm labourers. He also wore corduroy trousers and a waistcoat. He has a moderately broad chin, his lips are tightly compressed, and he possesses two deep lines coming from the nose to the corners of his mouth. These are generally taken to indicate a firmness of character. He has whiskers around his face and combs his hair down over a broad forehead'.

Superintendent Gillett was the first witness and he addressed the Mayor and said:

'Your worship, the prisoner here is David Coe, the man who is charged on suspicion with the murder of his nephew, John Coe.

Early yesterday morning the body of John Coe was found against a straw stack in a field on Canklow Road, about thirty yards from the fence. His head was broken in. Shortly afterwards the prisoner was seen hurrying away towards Brinsworth in a very excited condition. He was subsequently apprehended the same morning and brought to the police station'.

There was complete silence in the courtroom as the superintendent then produced the large hedgestake, which he said he believed it was the weapon with which the man had been killed. He said:

'this hedgestake was found and it appears to have blood on it and is supposed to have been used by the murderer, and to have been broken by the force of the blows. The prisoner was very forward in drink when he was apprehended. I only have now to ask for a formal remand until Thursday'.

A witness who swore had seen David Coe near the body on the morning of the murder, Mr George Goddard, was then sworn and he said:

'I live at Catcliffe and carry on my business at Rotherham. About a quarter to nine yesterday I was passing Canklow Mill and saw the prisoner there. He seemed to be in a very excited state, and was walking very fast. He seemed to be trying to get away from the area as quickly as possible'.

The prisoner was then formally remanded. Meanwhile the clothes of the deceased man and the prisoner, were taken for analysis to Dr Cobban, who by now had been able to microscopically examined the blood stains. He stated that he could confirm that the stains were blood, however he could not say for definite whether it was animal or human blood. However he promised that the spots were to be subjected to further examination. Superintendent Gillett gave evidence to state that after the body had been found, he had been informed that the victim had been seen in the company of John Henry Wood. He immediately sent his officers to bring the man to his house on Moorgate. It was near midnight however before Wood was found by Police Constable Ackroyd of Wickersley and Police Constable Bonnet of Whiston and brought to Superintendent

Gillett's private residence. Wood made his statement, and upon giving the superintendent a promise that he would attend the inquest if his expenses would be paid, he was released. Rumours immediately began to circulate the town that the Superintendent, having the man he thought was guilty locked away safely in one of his cells, took little notice of Woods statement. He was strongly criticised for his lack of action and even local newspapers were quickly commenting on the fact that the Rotherham police were reluctant to find anyone else guilty of the crime. The *Sheffield and Rotherham Independent* dated 21 March stated that:

'the police still adhere to the first opinion held, that David Coe, the man who is now in custody, and who it must be remembered is the uncle of the murdered man, is the real criminal. The only difficulty which remains to be disposed of, in their belief is the proceedings of the prisoner from five to six or seven on Thursday morning. The idea is firmly held that the murder was perpetrated early on Thursday morning'.

As it was by then common knowledge that David Coe had arrived at his aunts house at midnight on the night of the murder, and had left there at 5 am, he could not possibly be the murder.

Chapter Three: The Inquest

The inquest on the body of John Coe was held at the Rotherham Workhouse on Alma Road before coroner Mr Dossey Wightman on the afternoon of 20 February 1880. Before swearing in the jury the Coroner pointed out that he only intended to take evidence of identification of the body and the results of the post mortem. He would then adjourn the inquest until the following day. He explained that because the murder had only recently been carried out, the police were still making their enquiries into the case. The jury were then sworn in and went to view the body, still in the dead house of the workhouse. Dr Hardwicke accompanied the members of the jury and there he pointed out several of the injuries which the man had received. Returning back to the inquest the prisoner was brought into the room and he was described as 'not possessing the dejected and stupefied appearance that he had when first charged with the murder'. Now he was listening very carefully to the witnesses as they gave their evidence.

The first witness was the murdered mans' father, James Coe of Brinsworth. He pointed out that his son had never shown any violence to anyone, and therefore the reason for his murder was unknown. He was anxious to point out the gentleness that his son had always shown as he told the inquest:

'I am the father of the deceased, who was 26 years of age last month. He was a farm labourer and had been employed by Mr Thompson of Howarth Grange up to last Saturday night. As Mr Thompson had given up farming and gone to live in Warwickshire, my son was out of employment at the time of his death. He had no quarrel with Mr Thompson, any of his men, nor anyone at all on the premises at Haworth Grange. John had been lodging with me at the time he was working for Mr Thompson, and for the last six years, he came home to sleep at the house. I last saw him alive about 5 o'clock on Wednesday morning. At that time I got up to go to work and left him and his brother Harry in bed. I saw him go to bed on Tuesday night about half past nine. He was alright then, sober and apparently in good health. The next I heard was between 10 and 11 o'clock on Thursday when I was told that he had been

killed. My informant was Mrs Ann Badger of Brinsworth. I was working at Unwin's at White Hill Farm in the Tinsley parish, when I first became acquainted with the murder. I came at once to Rotherham Court House, but I did not see my son until this morning at the workhouse. I identified him as John Coe. The prisoner David Coe is my youngest brother and lives at Rotherham, but I do not know where. The prisoner is a labourer and I saw him last on Tuesday week near Masbro' station. I never spoke to him, nor do I converse with him at any time, for we are not good friends. My son John was a 'middling' good friend to him, and I never heard any quarrel between them. But I was never in their company when they were together. I know no one with whom my son John was at enmity. I never saw him quarrel with anyone'.

The next witness was Joseph Hawksworth, the man who had found the body. He told the Coroner that he worked at Mr Owen's foundry in Westgate and had known John Coe for twenty years or more. He explained that he and the deceased had been born and bred in Brinsworth, although he had not seen him for about a month or five weeks before his death. Hawksworth stated that about 8.10 am the morning of the 19 February, he had been walking along Canklow Road towards Rotherham when he came to a field belonging to Mr Jarvis containing a haystack. There he saw the body of a man lying about 25 yards away from the road. The body was lying with his head near the stack on the Rotherham side, and at first he was hesitant to approach because he suspected that the man was a tramp. He had found some tramps to be belligerent when approached and so he waited until two other men, father and son, John and George Swallow from Catcliffe, who he had passed earlier, had come up. They were followed by another man named Joseph Bentley who worked at Bentley Brewery who also looked into the field where the body was lying. The three men, at first argued whether or not the figure was the body of a man, but they agreed to climb through a hole in the hedge surrounding the field and find out. As they approached the body and saw all the blood they knew that it was indeed a man and that he had been murdered. Hawksworth told the inquest that he saw the man's hat where it lay a yard away from the body, but he had not immediately see the hedgestake. Although Hawksworth admitted that he had known John Coe well, he stated that he had not recognise the corpse, as the face and head were so bloody, swollen and distorted. He was therefore greatly surprised to be told later that the body he had found that morning was that of John Coe.

Medical evidence was then taken from Dr Hardwicke who stated that he had never treated the deceased man in his life to his knowledge. He said that a constable had called at his house about 9.10 am on the morning of the murder, and they had gone in a cab to Canklow Road. He described the way in which the body was lying. He said that the dead man had been laying with his back towards the stack and with his legs widely spread and his knees bent. His right hand rested upon his breast and his left hand was by his side. His face was covered in clotted blood and had froth around his mouth and there was a cut on the scalp over the left lateral part of the frontal bone. He found the limbs were all cold, although the abdomen was still slightly warm. At this point the coroner requested that a post mortem be carried out on the body and adjourned the inquest to the following day. At the reconvened inquest, Dr Hardwicke described the post mortem which he had undertaken that morning with Dr Cobban. The two surgeons had found the wound on the frontal bone which was about 1½ inches long. There was another bruise over the lower and anterior part of the same bone, and the bones of the nose presented a pulpy depressed appearance. When he removed the skull he found part of the brain was in the same pulpy condition and was surrounded by blood. There was also a small fracture running from the wound. The organs of the chest and abdomen were generally healthy and Dr Hardwicke stated that the cause of death was the fracture of the frontal bone of the skull. Ignoring the statements that some of the witnesses swore to the contrary, Dr Hardwicke gave his expert opinion that the man may have died as much as 9 or 10 hours earlier. Nevertheless he admitted that he could not state for certain.

Anxious at this point to rule out that such injuries could be caused accidentally, at this point the Coroner asked if such injuries could have been caused by a man falling down in a intoxicated state. Dr Hardwicke replied emphatically 'no I should say not sir'. He was asked if such injuries could have been caused if a drunken man might have fallen onto a hard surface, but again the surgeon stated that such a fall would not have caused such massive injuries.

Superintendent Gillett asked him if they could have been caused by the man falling off the stack of hay, but again Dr Hardwicke said that they could not. The Coroner then asked the surgeon if he had formed any opinion on how the murder had been committed and Dr Hardwicke stated that the hedgestake he had been shown would have been consistent as being a weapon which would inflict such terrible injuries. The Coroner asked him how many blows would it have taken to kill a normally healthy young man and the doctor replied it would take two or three heavy blows. He added that 'it would require great force to inflict those blows'. The foreman of the jury Mr James Tomlinson asked him if the blows would have caused an instant death, but Dr Hardwicke was unable to be certain on that point. One of the jury, a Mr Ryalls asked if a man could live for a while after receiving such a blow. The surgeon replied:

'quite possibly as long as portions of the brain would maintain the process of breathing and other necessary functions, the man may remain perfectly sensible although unable to move'.

Dr Cobban then took his place on the witness stand and concurred with all that Dr Hardwicke had said. He told the inquest that he had examined the deceased man's clothing and there were certain suspicious marks, although once again he was unable to say whether it was human blood or not. The Coroner told him that the clothing would be sent to an analyst and asked Superintendent Gillett to ensure that would be done, to which he agreed. Superintendent Gillett then asked for another adjournment until the following week. Almost as soon as the inquest was over and the people exited from the courtroom there was a buzz of conversation. The statement over the time of death made by Dr Hardwicke went against the witnesses statements that life was still in the body eight or nine hours later. Prior to the inquest, the police were acting on the supposition that the deed had been committed in the early hours of Thursday morning. Now the doctors evidence brought the time nearer to midnight when it was known that David Coe was at his aunt's house. The only other suspect was the man in whose company John Coe had been on the night he was murdered.

The funeral of the deceased man was held on Sunday 22 February 1880 at Tinsley Church. The night before the body had been brought from the workhouse to his home, and it was estimated that over two hundred people had gathered to watch the solemn procession, despite the fact that the weather was damp and cheerless. Once inside the house, the coffin was opened and the crowd availed themselves of a last chance to look at the dead man's features. Throughout the day a large concourse of spectators were seen going through the Coe's house anxious to pay their last respects to a man who had been nothing but kind and generous. On the day of the funeral it was reported that there were more than a thousand people in the churchyard, although once again the weather was cloudy and rainy. Many of the mourners were from the Catcliffe Lodge of the Oddfellows, of which John had been a member, whilst others were relatives and onlookers. The coffin was a simple one and bore an inscription which made no reference to the murder. It was simply inscribed 'John Coe, Died February 19th 1880. Aged 26 years'. The minister Rev. J F Butler performed the burial service and at the end he addressed the congregation stating that 'they were met together on a most solemn occasion, to commit to the last resting place the earthly remains of one who has been hurried out of this world'. He told them:

'A week ago neither you, nor I had any idea that one who has been often seen in this village would this afternoon have seen his body consigned to the grave. [...] When our poor brother left his home on Wednesday morning, he had no idea he would not return to it. Let us bear in mind we may be taken away just as suddenly'.

It was not only local people that took an interest in the murder. Over the next few days and weeks large numbers of sightseers from Rotherham, Sheffield and Doncaster visiting the area in Canklow where the atrocity had been committed. It was naturally assumed at this point that the attack had been motivated by robbery and that the victim's silver watch had not yet been found. The local newspapers took up this theme as they reported that:

'it is believed that the watch is bound up very closely with the murder, and the police are making every enquiry to discover its whereabouts, besides gathering together all the evidence they can'.

It was known that David Coe was always short of money, but his nephew had always been so generous and was known to have given him money on the day he died. However the local newspapers were soon putting the name forward of the other suspect in the case, that of John Henry Wood. As early as 20 February the *Sheffield and Rotherham Independent* were naming Wood as the possible murderer. That day's edition stated that:

'particulars gleaned by our representative, throw a different light on the whole circumstances, and point with a better show of reason to Wood as the perpetrator of the murder, rather than to the uncle Coe'

The 'particulars that had been gleaned' were that since the murder, a silver watch had been seen in the possession of Wood himself. Once that fact had been established, the Rotherham police finally issued a warrant for his arrest. But by then it was too late and John Henry Wood had disappeared.

Chapter Four: John Henry Wood

Contrary to John Coe respectable and amiable character, John Henry Wood had a history of petty thieving and was well known to the Rotherham police under his own name and his alias of Greaves. This despicable man even stole from his own parents and was arrested for the charge on 16 April 1877. What compounded the crime was that the purloined articles were of little value and included a black cloth coat, a waistcoat of his fathers and two of his mothers shawls from his home at Whiston. Wood was brought into custody where he admitted having stolen them and had pledged the items at three different pawn shops in Rotherham in order to evade detection. He was brought before the magistrates on 19 April where he was committed to take his trial at the Sheffield Intermediate Sessions on Thursday 30 April. After hearing all the evidence Wood was sentenced to four months imprisonment. The following November he was in court again, described as a labourer, charged with stealing a table cloth worth 9s 6d, the property of Walter Lee a quarry mason on 5 November. Wood had waited until the man and his wife were attending the Statute fair in Rotherham, before breaking into their house and taking the table cloth and other petty goods. He pawned them at the premises of Mr Lord of Henry Street, Rotherham. Wood was arrested and brought before the magistrates on 11 November 1878 where once again he was committed to take his trial. When he was brought before the Sheffield Michaelmas Intermediate Session on 28 November, John Henry Wood was given a 12 months prison sentence with hard labour. At the time of his trial a curious tale was circulating around the town of Rotherham regarding his strange behaviour. He had, at that time, been employed by Mr J D Styring of Whiston, when late one night Wood appeared at Mr Styring's house armed with a long iron bar or jemmy. He brandished the weapon vowing that he would not leave the premises until he had 'obtained some plunder'. Mr Styring was naturally very startled and immediately picking up a double barrelled shotgun, threw open the house door and invited Wood to enter. He promised him however that if he did so, he would empty his gun into him. Wood quickly departed and the next morning he went back to Mr Styring's house with his mother, and asked forgiveness for his actions the night before. His long suffering employer made no complaint and no action was taken against him. Nevertheless this incident gives us an insight into Woods impulsive behaviour which he acted upon thoughtlessly, indicating an inability to judge the outcome.

As we have seen, after the body of John Coe had been found and following the statement made, albeit incoherently by David Coe, police officers were ordered to bring Wood in for questioning. A search had been made for him and consequently it was midnight before he was taken before Superintendent Gillett. As we have seen at the time the Rotherham police were not taking Wood as a serious suspect, as David Coe was still in custody. In his statement Wood told the Superintendent that on the night of the murder after leaving the Chequers public house with the two Coe's, they walked along the highway towards Rotherham. When they left David Coe at Moorgate, he and the deceased man went past the Rotherham Independent College and called in for a drink at the Belvedere Inn, Moorgate and afterwards at the Butchers Arms, on Talbot Lane. From that place they went to Wellgate and having purchased a gallon of ale they then went to 'a house of questionable character' [a brothel] on Old Hill, Wellgate where they stayed for about an hour and a half. It is believed that the remains of Old Hill might be the little lane opposite the Mail Coach on Wellgate today. In the *Sheffield and Rotherham Advertiser* dated Saturday 6 March 1880 it was stated that Wood told the Superintendent that 'Coe went outside with one of the girls', whilst he stayed in the house. However he felt very uncomfortable because of the 'rough company'. Wood admitted that the two men were both the worse for the amount of beer they had drunk and that once he decided to leave, he called to Coe and the two men left the house. He admitted that at the time he was so drunk that he fell over a wall at the back. Wood told the Superintendent that eventually he left John at Wellgate before walking towards Broom, on his way home to Whiston. In his inebriated state he admitted that the only thing he could remember about that night was the following morning, when he woke up in a shed on Mr Leedham's farm premises at Broom. Rousing himself Wood then made his way to the Stag Inn on Wickersley Road where he arrived at some time between 8.30 and 9am. He was served by the landlord Henry Dawes who gave him a drink of ale and the some bread and cheese. Wood told Dawes that he had spent the night in a shed in one of Mr Leedham's fields. Soon afterwards the two men were joined by a quarry master named Charles Roberts and the three men sat together at the bar. At around 11 am more people entered the Stag and Ward was told that there had been a murder committed at Canklow. Soon after a man called Charles Young (alias Mills) entered and he also spoke about the murder. The landlord asked him if he knew the name of the victim, but Young stated that he did not know. Wood said that he remained at the Stag, drinking until 3 or 4 pm in the afternoon. Superintendent Gillett listened in silence to the mans statement and after asking Wood to sign it, he let him go. However Wood was advised by the Superintendent to attend the inquest the following day as he might be called as a witness. He agreed, providing his expenses would be paid, and then he went on his way.

On the afternoon of Friday 20 February Wood did indeed attend the inquest at the workhouse as he had been requested to do. Once the coroner stated that he had no intention of calling any witnesses that day, and just intended to identify the body however, Wood left. But the day after the inquest, there had been several reports around Rotherham that Wood had been seen with the silver watch in his possession. The landlord of the Stag Inn, Dawes had been interviewed and he told the officers that he had noticed that whilst Wood had been drinking at the Inn he was constantly playing with a watch. He also told them that Wood had paid for his drinks with a handful of silver and copper. Dawes also stated that he had heard Young ask Wood if he knew a man named Thomas Cliffe of Brinsworth who had been related to the victim. He described him as a man who had no hand just a hook and was employed a letter carrier. Wood said he did not know him. Dawes was unable to add any more to his statement at this point as the Stag was filling up with customers and he was busy serving beer to his customers. However he noted that Wood and Young went over to a corner table where he heard them discussing their joint experiences in Wakefield Prison. Other witnesses were saying that they had seen Wood with a watch and so when Superintendent Gillett heard that Wood had tried to fob the missing silver watch off on a man called Poynter the day after the murder, he sent officers to arrest him. However by the time they arrived at the house of Wood's parents it was found that he had now gone to ground. A description was given of the wanted man in the *Sheffield and Rotherham Independent* of Wednesday 25 February 1880 which read:

'He is 27 years of age of slim build, 5 feet 6½ inches in height and was dressed when last seen in a light drab suit, somewhat worn and wearing a black felt hat. His complexion is rather pallid, with a firm face, very light hair, closely cropped and a slight moustache of the same colour. He has also a cut - not very deeply marked - over one eye'.

Local people of Rotherham heard on the morning of February 24 1880 that a warrant had been issued for the arrest of John Henry Wood. When rumours told about the fact that Wood had been seen with the dead man's watch, suspicions had been confirmed that the watch would eventually lead to the perpetrator of the crime. However what also incensed the inhabitants of the town was the fact that days after the reports of the stolen watch had been circulating, that David Coe was still in the prison cells charged with being his nephew's killer. The newspapers were openly critical of the methods used by the Rotherham police and it was suggested that once they had a suspect in their clutches, they were desperate to find some evidence against him, rather than establish the truth of the matter. The *Sheffield and Rotherham Advertiser* dated 25 February, a week after the murder and three days after Wood had been seen with the watch, stated:

'The Rotherham police have not as yet been afforded any further opportunity of displaying their ability and discernment with respect to the murder committed within the borough on Thursday last. The man Coe is still in custody, but from the facts which now appear to be seen in their true light by the authorities, a gross mistake has been committed in setting the man Wood at liberty last week. Suspicion strongly attaches itself to him, and the police armed with a warrant, are now striving to secure his re-capture'.

David Coe's statement made the day after his arrest, made it very clear that he was not with his nephew when he was killed. According to the evidence of Dr Hardwicke John Coe had been killed around midnight, yet David Coe had been at the house of his aunt at that time and therefore had a very strong witness to his innocence. The fact was that he was still in custody resulted in strong feeling among the people of the town. These were quickly picked up by the local reporters who wrote that:

'The murder of John Coe and the vain efforts of the police to trace the person who committed the crime, were almost general topics of conversation in Rotherham yesterday, and the conduct of the police was strongly commented upon by the inhabitants'.

By this time police authorities had clear evidence that the day after the murder, Wood had offered to sell the silver watch to a man called Robert Poynter, who was a farm servant in the employ of Mr Mudie of Royds Moor, Whiston. On that afternoon following the murder, Poynter told police officers that he was on his way home after finishing work. He was walking along Broom Road near to Mr Leedham's farm, leading a horse and cart at sometime between 4 and 5 pm. Suddenly he saw a man coming towards him from the direction of the Stag Inn, and as the man came nearer he recognised John Henry Wood. Pointer noted that Wood looked like he had spent most of the day at the Inn, although he claimed he was steady enough as he walked. Poynter asked him what he was doing and why he was not working. Wood told him that he had been on 'a bit of a spree' and if he had met him nearer the public house, they could have had a beer together. Wood then produced a silver watch and told him 'I am not hard up yet, and when I have spent the money I can always pop [pawn] this and get some more'. He urged Poynter to buy it, but the man had no money on him, although he asked to see the watch, and Wood gave it to him to examine. Poynter later told the police that he noted that the watch was made of silver, with a white dial but the curb chain was made of steel and its hands were set at either just before or just after 2 am. Wood then took it out of his hands and attempted to wind it up, but without success. Just for a joke Poynter asked Wood to 'lend it to him until he could afford to pay for it'. Wood told him that he would, but warned him not 'to let our old fellow or our old woman know about it', meaning his mother and father. Pointer stated that they then had some other conversation before parting and going in different directions, Wood going towards Rotherham and Poynter continuing along Broom Road to his home. Poynter thought no more about it until he read about the murder of John Coe the day before, and realised that it was the very same silver watch which had belonged to the murdered man. The next day he took the watch back to Wood at his fathers house. When Wood saw Poynter he said 'Did you think it was his watch Bob' meaning the murdered man. Poynter replied 'I don't know what to think Jack'. Wood told him 'you must not say anything Bob, you must keep it quiet' but Poynter noted that Wood did not appear calm or excited as he gave him back the watch.

Once it was revealed that Wood had disappeared, people of the town were asking, why if Wood was truly innocent of the murder as he had claimed, had he disappeared. His friends stated they had no knowledge of his whereabouts and it was reported that the police were now searching the woods and fields around Whiston for him. Throughout the day of 25 February, there had been a report that he had been seen in Whiston and he was thought to be hiding in the locality of Royds Moor. The excitement in Rotherham grew to fever pitch as people congregated in front of the Town Hall anxious to gain any information on the man now thought to be the murderer. It was reported that for hours people stayed outside the Town Hall hoping to be rewarded by the latest gossip on the search, or better still, a glimpse of Wood being arrested by officers. They were rewarded by hearing that the day before Wood had crept from his place of concealment at noon and had been given a share of a labourers dinner, in a field not far from Whiston. The man who gave Wood some of his bread was Thomas Yeardley who was working on a hedge for his master Mr Charles Foers. He had indeed seen the wanted man come out of a field and creep along the side of the hedge, where he loitered about until he and another labourer engaged on the same job, decided to sit down and have their dinner. Wood then came up to them and asked the other labourer for 'a bit to eat'. It was reported that Wood was wearing a very long black or blue coat, a felt hat and appeared to be very haggard and forlorn. He told the two men that he had nothing to eat since Sunday. The other man gave Wood some bread and bacon which he ate greedily. When he finished Wood looked at Yeardley and asked him if he too could spare something, and he gave him some bread. Wood thanked them both and then asked them what the news was in Whiston and as the men admitted that there was a lot of talk about the murder. Wood told them that he had been with John Coe on the night of the murder and they had been at 'Big Liz's' but there were a lot of rough men there and as a consequence they soon left. He concluded that he had left Coe at Wellgate and he had slept that night at Leedham's farm. All the time he was talking, it was reported that Wood kept looking very uneasily around him as if expecting any moment to be surprised by the police. He did not eat the second piece of bread which Yeardley had given him, but put it into his pocket for later. As he left he told the two men that if he was not apprehended in the meantime, he intended to be at the adjourned inquest to be held on John Coe.

Rumours continued to flow around Rotherham on sightings of the wanted man. One report had it that Wood had been seen in Bent Lane just that morning, and had conversed with a man employed as a stone breaker. Another alarm was also given that he had been seen at Brampton prowling around, and several constables under Sergeant Martin Sykes went to search the area. Further report continued to be heard that the fugitive had been seen eating turnips out of a field near a farm owned by a man called Roberts, as well as others stating that he had sought refuge in a local quarry. However all the sightings came to nothing as the wanted man continued to evade the police. Yet witnesses still reported seeing him. When Mr Roberts heard that the police were searching his farm, he took out his double barrelled gun and helped them in their search. It was later reported that at the time they were searching the farm, Wood had been spotted at Laughton-en-le-Morthern. It was acknowledged that the police would have difficulty in catching Wood, who was reported to be:

'very fleet of foot and leading the police who were looking for him a right merry dance, playing hide and seek with them very successfully'.

This was due to the fact that when Wood had once before gone on the run from the police, he managed to keep himself hidden for a month. Local people knew that he was used to sleeping out in sheds and haystacks as his alibi had revealed. On the previous occasion when Wood was finally captured he seemed to be no worse for his adventure. Local people became desperate to hear the latest news on Wood and large crowds continued to collect around the Town Hall. So many sighting were heard of seeing the fugitive that the *Sheffield and Rotherham Independent* of February 27 doubted their veracity. It claimed that:

'Whiston People are perpetually coming into Rotherham and saying that they have either just seen, or know someone who has just seen Wood. Apparently many of them enjoy the fun of giving the police as much trouble as possible. The opinion is gradually gaining ground in the town that the statements relative to Wood being seen so frequently during the last few days, have simply been set afloat to throw the police off the scent, and that by those means it is likely Wood may have got clean away from the immediate district'.

The police authorities however were determined to catch Wood which resulted in fourteen officers, four Sergeants and ten constables, being given the massive task of searching isolated areas around Rotherham. The same night that the burial of the victim was being held at Tinsley, Sergeant Sykes of the Laughton district and the men under his command spent the whole of the night scouring the neighbourhoods of Brampton, Ulley and Whiston. They searched all the woods and buildings around Wickersley, all the old quarries and every haystack from there back to Rotherham. They also made a special search of Mr Leedham's farm, at Broom where Wood was frequently known to hide. Over the next four days and nights the men were kept at it, often working a fourteen hour shift without a break in order to catch Wood. They searched all the areas around Carr, Stainton, Maltby and Bramley and as a result, by Thursday night all the men engaged in the hunt were reported to be tired and weary. Consequently Superintendent Gillett sent the men home for a rest. It was known that after his drinking spree following the murder, that Wood had little money on him when he went on the run. However what also had to be taken in account was the fact that he was a very determined man, who would starve to death before allowing himself to be arrested for the murder. Nevertheless sightings of Wood continued to be brought to the attention of the police, Even after some officers had been sent home for a rest, reports continued to be received. When it was reported that he had been seen in Badsley Moor Lane in

Rotherham, two policemen in plain clothes were quickly dispatched to the area. As it was a very bright moonlit night, hopes were quite high that he would be swiftly captured, but once again, if it had been Wood, the man had gone to ground.

Nevertheless, despite all the continued sightings and the belief that David Coe was not guilty of the murder, he continued to be held in the prison cells a week after he had been charged. By 25 February his solicitor, Mr Parker Rhodes wrote to Superintendent Gillett the following letter:

'February 25 1880
Sir, On behalf of David Coe, the man now in custody, we must ask that if there is any evidence against him, it must be produced before the justices before any further remand is granted. If there is no evidence the man should be discharged.
PS The information we have collected seems to establish beyond a doubt that David Coe had nothing to do with the murder of John Coe. All the information we have is at your service, and if it will afford you any assistance in detecting the real culprit we shall be very glad to produce it, Yours etc., BADGER, RHODES & Co.'

The police and legal authorities realised that something must be done, so later that same afternoon David Coe was brought before the magistrates. He was remanded at large pending further enquiries and he, no doubt gratefully, finally left the police station. Superintendent Gillett then responded to Mr Parker Rhodes by informing him that David Coe had been released on bail. However David Coe's solicitor felt that was not good enough, and that for the sake of his client's good character he should have been discharged of the crime altogether, rather than released 'at large'. After some discussion it was agreed by the magistrates that the whole subject would be left until after the coroners inquest had been concluded. It was asserted on all sides that, with the exception of the Rotherham police force, no one in the town believed in David Coe's guilt. When Mr Parker Rhodes again went to the police court and demanded that his client be totally discharged rather than being given bail, he stated that 'was not a proper position for a man to be placed in, especially as no evidence had been made against him'. The magistrates told the solicitor that they considered the remanding at large to be the equal of a discharge.

All these details were reported in local newspaper and avidly read by local people of the town anxious to learn every single detail of the crime. The fact that Coe had been bailed rather than discharged still rankled with many people of the town. The *Sheffield and Rotherham Independent* dated 27 February 1880 recognised this discontent and reported that the bench:

'were justified in their refusal, as opposed to the ostrich like policy of Superintendent Gillett who had, metaphorically, his head in the sand when he allowed Wood to walk away a few days ago. It is rather singular that nearly everybody in the Rotherham district other than the police thought that John Henry Wood was implicated in the murder of John Coe, and that David Coe, the young man's uncle, was innocent'.

Both local gossip and newspaper reports were openly critical of police methods. Even national newspapers picked up on the subject. The *York Herald* dated 25 February also criticised the Rotherham police force when it stated that:

'Since the murder of John Coe at Rotherham last Thursday the inhabitants of the town and neighbourhood have been loudly protesting against the non-apprehension by the police of John Henry Wood, alias Greaves, who was the last person in the company of the deceased. It will be remembered that almost immediately after the discovery the murder the police apprehended the uncle of the deceased David Coe, on suspicion of being the perpetrator of the deed, and since then they have been trying to get up evidence in support of their theory. The public however, were almost unanimously against them, and it now appears that these officials have somewhat changed their opinion'.

The following day in another reference to the merry dance being led by Wood, the same newspaper stated that matters uncovered so far 'affirm that whilst the police were going about pretty much in a body, the suspected one [Wood] played hide and seek with them very successfully'. Thankfully Wood would not remain at large for very much longer!

Chapter Five: The Capture of Wood and the Second Inquest

On the morning of 27 February 1880, Sergeant Sykes and Police constable Partridge and other officers dressed in plain clothing resumed the hunt for the wanted man, and by 11 am they and their men had searched the area around Ulley and Brampton Common. The sergeant was reported to be wearing a fisherman's worsted cap, a white loose smock and corduroy trousers, whilst Partridge wore clothes which an unemployed artisan seeking work might wear. The men had got as far as Dinnington when they heard of a sighting of the fugitive at Woodsetts. A local clergyman, Rev. G Athorp placed his coachman, horse and trap at the service of the two exhausted men and they set off. At approximately 2.30 pm they were about 13 miles from Rotherham on a turnpike road leading to Woodsetts via Cotteril Wood, when they saw a group of men coming towards them. One of them was acting very suspiciously with his coat collar turned up and his shoulders hunched. A man called Samuel Pond who Sykes knew in the group, told the Sergeant that he did not know the man he indicated, who was a stranger. Sykes immediately jumped out and grabbed the man by the collar of his coat. The fugitive said to him 'alright I know what you want me for'. The sergeant arrested him on suspicion of being involved in the murder of John Coe at Rotherham, and also with stealing the watch, but Wood immediately replied 'I never had a watch in my life, and those who say so are liars'. He was then handcuffed to PC Partridge and put into the trap. It was reported that at the time of his arrest, Wood was trembling like a leaf. As they drove away one of the other men shouted to Wood 'mind thy neck or else Marwood would get hold of thee'. This was a reference to William Marwood the executioner. The men in the trap immediately went to Laughton-en-le-Morthern police office, where the fugitive begged for some food. All the men had something to eat and drink before heading triumphantly towards Rotherham. All the time they had been in the police office, the news of Woods arrest had been circulating around the village of Laughton. Consequently by the time the party set off there was quite a crowd of inhabitants which turned out, curious to see the man the police had been desperately looking for. Nervously Wood watched the large crowd and he seemed afraid. He asked Sykes to try to disguise him somehow and the sergeant told him that once they got to Broom, about a mile south east of Rotherham, they would do something. Consequently as they approached the town they placed Wood on the bottom of the trap and covered him with blankets. By this manner when they reached the door of the Town Hall, Wood was able to scramble unseen into the Police Office with great speed. Although College Square had been crowded for many nights past, on that particular occasion, being 7 pm it was very quiet, although such peace was not to last. Within just a few hours, news of his capture had circulated through the town and the Town Hall steps were literally besieged. On occasions it required the efforts of two or three constable to restrain the crowd and to ensure the steps were kept clear.

It was reported that by the time the men reached the police station in Rotherham Wood was again complaining of being hungry. On the journey he told the officers that over the last few days, he had been unable to get much food, and had spent most nights getting what sleep he could in hedge bottoms. When Wood heard about all the sightings that had been made of him, he roared with laughter. He stated that he had left Whiston on Monday and had passed through Anston and had never been anywhere near his home, or on the Rotherham side of Whiston since that time. Therefore all the sightings of him in that area were false. He also denied the statement of Yeardley that he had shared his dinner with him. All the food he had obtained he had begged as he passed along. Continuing with his account, Wood said that on the previous night he had slept near some limekilns in the vicinity of Cotterill Wood Farm, Woodsetts. Having gone to the farm about 6 am he saw two or three men preparing to do some threshing work on the farm. The men were making a fire in the engine boiler prior to getting up the necessary steam to drive the machine. Wood had asked if there was any work, but the men told him that other men had just been engaged to do the threshing. The men took pity on him however when they saw how cold he was, and as they were about to have breakfast they invited him to look after the fire. When they returned, he told them that he was used to farm work and came from Whiston. Just then the owner of the farm came up to see how they were getting on and Wood disappeared. The men told the farmer that they suspected that the man was probably the fugitive Wood, and he passed on the information to the local officer who gave it to Sergeant Sykes and Police Constable Partridge.

Meanwhile in Rotherham the adjourned inquest into the murder of John Coe was opened by the Coroner, Mr. Dossey Wightman at the Workhouse that same morning at 10.30 am. It was expected that due to the great interest in the case over the last few days, that the second inquest at the workhouse would be a lengthy one. When the coroner announced that the only witness was to be David Coe however, the members of the jury appeared reluctant to bring the inquiry to a close. Coe attended with his solicitor Mr Parker Rhodes and it was not long before he returned to the question of the status of David Coe. Mr Parker Rhodes told the inquest that his client had been 'remanded at large' and that subsequently no suspicions could now be attached to him. The coroner agreed and stated that he would therefore just take the evidence of his client, but he could not speak for the magistrates as he was unsure of what course they intended to take. However it was simply the duty of the inquest jury to establish by what means John Coe had met his death. Mr Wightman clarified that there was not a shadow of doubt that Coe had been killed, and that he must have been murdered by someone. Therefore after hearing David Coe's evidence, he should he continue to adjourn the proceedings for an unlimited time until:

'the affair was ripe enough for further consideration at the jury's hands. As things rested at the moment the magistrates are not in a position to indict the person responsible for the death of John Coe'

The coroner concluded that unless the jury had any suggestions to the contrary, he would take the evidence of David Coe and close the enquiry. However the foreman of the jury, Mr James Tomlinson had something to say. He asked the coroner if Dr Hardwicke, who was present at the inquest, could establish the death of John Coe a bit nearer than the 9 or 10 hours, he had previously stated, and whether that was still his opinion. Dr Hardwicke, who had not expected to be called as a witness yet again, took the stand. He reminded the jury that at the time of giving his evidence, he had stated that he could not speak with any certainty as to the exact time of death and as to that nothing had changed. Mr Tomlinson then asked the surgeon if it was possible that the deceased was killed much later and suggested about 5 am? Dr Hardwicke flatly denied this, stating that was simply not consistent with the temperature of the body of the deceased man. The coroner added that the body temperature would also have been affected by the weather if it was a cold day, and also whether the victim had been a fat or thin man. Dr Hardwicke said that stiffening comes over a dead body from between 10 to 24 hours afterwards, and in this case the mans arms were beginning to get stiff. Therefore he had no option but to stick with his first statement, although, as he had stated at the time, he could not speak with any degree of certainty. The foreman of the jury Mr Tomlinson then asked if the witness Mr Hall would be giving evidence to clarify that he had seen Wood's leg move. Dr Hardwicke stated that at the time Hall would have been 35 yards away and therefore it was difficult to understand how he had seen the mans leg move. The coroner at this point interjected. He told the foreman and the other members of the jury that in his experience that:

'when a man has been murdered the witnesses were generally somewhat excited, and although they without doubt intended to speak the truth, they contradicted each other in some of the details wonderfully. I should say in all probability that the man did not move at all'.

The surgeon was then asked if he could say whether Coe had been attacked standing or lying down, but Dr Hardwicke stated that too was hard to judge. The foreman explained that his object was to try to determine the way in which the deceased had been hit. If he had been killed whilst he was asleep, or whether a quarrel or a fight had taken place between the parties at the time of the murder. Mr Tomlinson said if they knew the answer, it could make the difference between a murder or a manslaughter verdict. The coroner explained that according to the evidence previously given by Dr Hardwicke, the victims skull had been battered in and reduced to a pulpy condition. This was indicative of a vicious attack, in his opinion blows given in a quarrel would not result in such serious injuries. David Coe then repeated his statement of what had happened on the day of the murder, and concluded by stating, yet again, that he had left the deceased and Wood together.

At this point the coroner told the inquest that he would now conclude the enquiry, subject to the jury's approval, and the only question they had to answer was how John Coe came to his death. However the good men of Rotherham on the jury panel were reluctant to conclude the inquest without a mention of the man now in custody. The foreman, Mr Tomlinson interrupted him and stated 'I am sorry to say I am not satisfied with the matter'. The coroner would not be moved and stated that at that time there was not enough evidence showing who had committed the murder. He reminded the jury, showing some impatience, that the best course to take was to leave it in the hands of the magistrates. Another member of the jury Mr Rylands also wanted to bring Wood into the enquiry and said that 'there is a person who has possession of the murdered man's watch' and requested that he might be brought into court. The coroner stated that at that time he had no evidence against anyone and had no way of following that matter up. Once again he told the jury that they could return what verdict they thought proper, and if they were averse to concluding the inquest, he could adjourn it again. Nevertheless he added it would be more advisable to say simply how John Coe came to his death, and to leave the authorities to ascertain who was the guilty person. He added that the magistrates would then have the power to send the guilty man for trial at the assizes. Two of the jurymen, Mr Lomas and Mr Henry Turner agreed, but Mr Tomlinson said that the week before, the coroner had said that the duty of the jury was to be called together to enquire by what person or persons John Coe had come to his death. The coroner told them that their first duty was to decide how the deceased man had met his death and during that enquiry, if it were disclosed who had caused the death, they would have to bring in a verdict accordingly. He was aware that the capture of Wood had been widely reported and warned the jury that they had to be guided by what evidence was given in the inquest, and not by what they had heard outside. Mr Rylands stated that had the jury been in the possession of the statement which the prisoner Wood had made to Superintendent Gillett the week before, they would have ordered him to be locked up at once. In fact they only heard of the statement on the morning after the inquest had been adjourned, when a warrant for Woods arrest had been issued. Mr Wightman, argued that it was the duty of the magistrates to go into the case more thoroughly, and the jury were only required to make the decision of whether the verdict on the death of John Coe was manslaughter or murder. He stated therefore the only question for this jury was 'were they satisfied in their own minds, according to the evidence of Dr Hardwicke, that the man had been murdered'. Mr Rylands agreed that he was satisfied that the man had been murdered. The coroner then said that if the jury were satisfied that John Coe had been murdered by person or persons unknown, they must leave the matter there, as it was quite certain that the evidence did not justify them in saying who had committed the murder. The coroner then requested the jury to say if they agreed with the verdict he had suggested. They all finally replied in the affirmative, and the inquest was then concluded with the verdict being that John Coe had met his death 'murdered by some person or persons unknown'.

Like the jury, the verdict of the adjourned inquest did not sit well with many people of the town who were now openly critical of the coroner, who they felt had exceeded in his duty. One reporter claimed that the evidence at the inquest disclosed little beyond what the people of Rotherham had already known. He reported that he also felt that some of the jury wanted to exceed their own duty and name the guilty man, before he had been tried and convicted. He felt that certain members of the jury appeared to be loath to bring the proceedings to a close, and stated:

'It did not appear to some of the jury that to have ascertained by what means the deceased came by his death was all that was required of them. They seemed to consider it their duty to discover by whom the murder had been committed. The coroner however cleared the difficulty up by pointing out the exact duty required of them'.

However little did they know that yet another witness was, at that moment, being interviewed by the Rotherham police force. A cabman called William Holmes had reported to the police that on the night of the murder he had been waiting outside a Gentlemen's Club in the High Street when he saw Wood and John Coe walking together. As Wood had told the police that he had left Coe at the bottom of Wellgate, this was seen to be yet another blatant lie. As they passed the cabman Holmes overheard one of them say to the other that 'they would make the beggars pay for it'. Then having picked up the fare, he was taking him to West House, along Canklow Road when he saw the two men again. On Saturday 28 February the cabman identified Wood, who had been placed in a line-up among 12 other individuals in the Rotherham police cells, with little difficulty. Even though Wood had finally been tracked down and arrested, the watch and chain belonging to the dead man was still missing and the Rotherham Police were known to be very anxious to trace it. Not unnaturally they turned to the best form of information gathering, the local press and offered an award of £10 for any information. The *Sheffield and Rotherham Independent* of 1 March 1880 had a notice which read:

'We have been requested to state that anyone who has the watch in their care, would meet with the gratitude of the police officials if they would hand it over to them. It is an ordinary sized silver Geneva watch, with consular case and a white enamelled dial. Engraved on the dome of the movement was "No 41,907" and "J G Needham, Rotherham". Attached to the watch is a medium sized steel curb, and plated oval swivel seal, with imitation bloodstone set into it.'

Many people were now confident that the watch would soon by in the hand of the local police force, and the mystery surrounding the death of John Coe would be finally be solved.

Chapter Six: Magistrates Court Appearances.

On Thursday 28 February 1880 for most of the day people had again gathered in the streets around the Town Hall entrance, anxious to get a glimpse of John Henry Wood. So big were the crowds that Superintendent Gillett gave orders that the doors were to be kept locked and they were rigorously guarded by two constables. Instead of dispersing however, the crowd simply collected at the gates leading to Inspector Hammonds residence, still hoping to see Wood as he passed from his cell into the police office. They were unlucky however as a very strict watch was kept on the prisoner, as the police were determined not to lose him, now he had been finally captured. Two other minor cases of begging and assault were heard by the magistrates, before Wood was brought in from the police cells at 11.55am. Although there was much excitement as the prisoner was placed in the courtroom, the proceedings were destined to be short and sweet. Wood was placed before the Mayor, Alderman Harrison and the ex-Mayor, Alderman Wigfield where it was reported that he was still wearing the same clothes that he had been found in. The prisoner's face still showed a pinched look, as if in evidence that he had been a long time without any food. He was charged with the wilful murder of John Coe and the theft of the stolen watch. Mr Parker Rhodes outlined the case for the prosecution. He said:

'In this case your Worship, I am instructed to prosecute, and therefore all I intend to do today is to ask you to formally to remand John Henry Wood alias Greaves, who is charged with the murder of John Coe, until next week. I propose to simply ask for that remand upon the sworn information which is already before you, and not to produce any further evidence, until the man is brought up on Thursday'.

The Mayor addressing the prisoner told him that he would be remanded until the following week, and Wood did not make any reply before being marched back to the cells. Finally David Coe was eliminated from police enquiries. He was brought before the Rotherham magistrates on Tuesday 2 March and formally discharged on the warrant which had charged him with the murder of John Coe of Brinsworth on 18 February. Now that he had been released the people of the town heard the news that they had been waiting for and they were delighted.

On Thursday 4 March when the doors to the court room were finally thrown open, a large swell of people entered, and within just a few moments the room was packed. Wood was defended by Mr W E Clegg. Throughout the enquiry the prisoner seemed to be most unconcerned and stood in the dock with his hands folded on the ledge of the dock. Mr Parker Rhodes described how Wood and the deceased man had continued into Rotherham after leaving David Coe behind. He listed the number of public houses they had called in on the way. The Belvedere, the Butchers Arms, the Pack Horse and from thence to the Mail Coach where they were joined by two prostitutes known as Elizabeth Saunders (aka 'Big Liz') and Annie Wilks. In all the pubs John Coe had been very liberal with his money, paying for beer and whiskey and also for a gallon of beer which he and Wood took to Saunders house on Old Hill, Wellgate. Mr Rhodes then related how the two men sat on a sofa at the house and it was noticed and commented on the fact that Wood now had in his possession the peeled stick. The prosecution pointed out that this was the same stick that had been found at the side of the dead body the next morning. After only a short while Coe came out of Big Liz's house, followed by Wood and both were heard falling over a wall just outside the house. Mr Rhodes described the cabman in the High Street seeing the two men and overhearing their conversation, before his final sighting of them about 400 yards from where the body was found. Mr Rhodes told the magistrates that the cabman had successfully identified Wood at the police station. He stated that the next day Wood was seen as various public houses including the Stag Inn on Wickersley Road, where he was seen repeatedly taking out and looking at a silver watch, shaking it and putting it to his ears. Several times Wood tried to turn the hands with his fingers, but seemed unable to make the watch work. The prosecution emphasized that this was the same watch which Coe's relatives had stated as being that which belonged to the deceased man. It was easily identifiable due to the marks on the back which Coe had made when opening it with a knife.

Joseph Hawksworth was the next witness and he told the coroner:

'I am a moulder living at Catcliffe and working at Mr Owen's foundry, Wheathill, Rotherham. On Thursday morning, the 19th instant I was going from Catcliffe to my work, taking the road at the bottom of Canklow Wood towards Rotherham. I know a straw stack on that road belonging to John Jarvis, a little way from the road. I was going along past the stack at about 8.20 am and noticed something which eventually turned out to be the dead body of John Coe, who appeared to have been murdered. I Joseph Bentley and John Swallow went up to where the man was, and found his face covered in blood. The head was nearest the stack, with the feet outwards from it. Swallow went forward and gave information to the police of what we had seen. Next morning I saw the dead body at the workhouse. The face had been washed and I recognised it as that of John Coe'

Sergeant Thomas Morley described finding the body and the wounds which had been inflicted on him. He stated:

'I noticed a large wound on the top of the left temple, rather high up, and above the nose a small hole as if the forehead had been bulged in. Blood was oozing from his ears and the wounds I unfastened his clothes and placed my hand on his abdomen which was very warm'

Sergeant Morley searched the pockets of the dead man and found two knives, a catapult, a piece of India rubber, a pipe, an iron washer, a piece of string and a button. However he found no money or watch on the man's person. He described the scene and finding the hedge stick about 20 feet from the body, which he delivered to Mr Alfred Henry Allen at Sheffield for analysis. He also then produced the peeled stick which he found about five feet from the body, among the straw. The sergeant stated that he had remained by the body until the arrival of Dr Junius Hardwicke. When Morley was cross examined he told the magistrates that there did not appear to be any signs of a struggle having occurred near the stack, although the grass and hay had been very trampled. He complained that there were already many people at the stack when he arrived, and they were crowding around the body and trampling the grass which hid any signs of a struggle. Dr Hardwicke gave his evidence describing the wounds in detail and concluding that 'it would require considerable violence to cause such wounds. Once again he re-iterated that in his opinion the man had been dead for nine or ten hours. He was followed by Mr Alfred Henry Allen who introduced himself as the public analyst for the West Riding of Yorkshire, North Derbyshire and the borough of Sheffield. He gave his evidence of receiving the two pieces of hedge stick on the 21 February from Sergeant Morley. On the 28 February he received a hat, coat, shirt and waistcoat from Sergeant Sykes. Allen described find blood on the stake, the right wristband of the dead mans shirt and on the right sleeve of his coat, but concluded that 'it is not possible for anyone to say with certainty in the case of dried blood stains whether it be human blood'. However he had compared it to his own blood and that 'in every character it exactly agreed with my own blood'. There was also straw chaff on the slim stick, which had been found about five feet from the body.

The mother of the deceased man, Mrs Ann Coe described her son leaving the house on the morning of the 18 February and not seeing him again until she saw the dead body at the workhouse. She described the silver watch and how he 'used to wear it always' and stated how he wound it up on the night of the 17th before going to bed. Mrs Coe said how the watch was dented due to him opening the back with a knife, and how she had bought the watch for him from Mr Needham's shop on College Street, Rotherham. She was followed by her husband who concurred with her evidence and stated that how 'the man Cliffe married my sister. He has one hand taken off and now wears a hook'. Several other witnesses then gave evidence of seeing the two Coe's together at the Chequers Inn and the landlord Robert Elliott said that the two men seemed to be on the best of terms with each other. He described how John Coe ordered a drink and proffering half a sovereign as payment. Wood entered the public house and John Coe offered him a drink which he paid for, and Wood sat at the same table as the two Coe's and saw the change being given to him in return for the drinks. David Coe then gave his evidence and there was complete silence in the court as he spoke. He said:

'I am a farm labourer and I live at 61 Henry Street, Rotherham and John Coe was my nephew. We followed the hounds together at Wickersley on the 18th and afterwards went to the Chequers where we had some refreshment. I saw Edward Wilkinson at the Chequers and both he and my nephew carried sticks, which they exchanged. Wood, who I knew by the name of Greaves, was at the Chequers and he walked with us to Moorgate. I did not go any further with them and I have not seen the prisoner since, until today, nor did I see John Coe alive again'.

He described staying at Mrs Roddis's house and stated that he was not very drunk. He said that he knew Wood and his nephew knew him slightly, before concluding that he had never heard of any quarrel or bad feeling between them.

Robert Hill the publican of the Belvedere Inn on Moorgate told the magistrates that Wood and John Coe were in his public house on the evening of the 18th, and the next day Wood entered again with a man called Fred Grey. When Hill asked Wood who he came in with the previous night the prisoner admitted that it was Jack Coe and the publican told him 'that's the man that has been murdered'. At that time a policemen was in the house making enquiries about the murder and when he heard Wood admit that he had been with the victim the night before, he came over to talk to him. The officer asked Wood where he had gone after leaving the Belvedere the previous night and Wood told him 'we went to Big Liz's'. Once again he said that he had left the deceased man at Wellgate and that he had 'not known of the murder above five minutes'. Hill told the enquiry that as Wood spoke to the police officer it seemed to the publican that he was very excited.

Thomas Wright, a puddler of 11 College Road, Rotherham spoke of being in the Pack Horse, Wellgate at 9.30 pm when Wood came into the house with another men. The three men then went to the Mail Coach and they were having a drink there when Big Liz entered. A woman called Annie came in later and eventually they all went to Big Liz's taking a gallon of beer with them for which John Coe paid about 11 pm. Wright noted that Wood's companion had a silver watch which he saw him consult frequently. He described the two men as being sober and not quarrelsome, but when they left they were 'half and half' but seemed to be on good terms. He stated that they remained at the brothel until about 20 minutes past 11. He said that the man he later knew to be Coe left first and soon afterwards was followed by Wood.

Elizabeth Saunders, otherwise known as 'Big Liz' then gave her evidence, which indicated that by that time, Wood had possession of the stick which Coe had swapped with Edward Wilkinson. She said:

'I am a married woman, living away from my husband at Old Hill, Wellgate. I remember going into the Mail Coach and saw the prisoner Wood and another man whom I did not know. After being there some time, I, the two men mentioned, Thomas Wright and Annie Wilks went across to my house, and a big bottle full of beer was taken across. Wood let a stick fall twice and, and it was picked up the first time by Wilks and then by me. Wood was also in possession of the stick at my house. Both Wood and the dead man were together on my sofa. Coe was the first to leave and Wood followed soon afterwards, having the stick referred to in his hand at the time'.

When she was cross examined on the kind of house she kept, she boldly told the coroner 'I keep a brothel'. She was followed by Annie Wilks who also told the magistrates:

'I am a single woman, living at the house of the last witness. While I was in Elizabeth Saunders house, the prisoner dropped his stick. I picked it up and asked him to give it to me for Elizabeth Saunders little boy, but he did not comply. The dead man left first and Wood followed, taking the stick with him. The next evening I went to the Rotherham Workhouse and was shown a dead body, which was that of Coe, who had been at Saunders house and had been with the prisoner. The next time I saw the stick it was at Superintendent Gillett's office, and I picked that out from a lot of others that I have recognised today'.

Next came the evidence of one of the last men to see the prisoner and his victim alive, so his evidence was crucial in giving the lie to Woods statement that he left the deceased at Wellgate. It was

43

William Holmes, the cab driver of Talbot Lane, Rotherham who spoke of seeing the two men together, as he waited outside the Gentlemen's Club on the High Street. He said:

'I remember the night of the 18th alt. I was standing with my cab opposite the club in High Street, waiting to convey two of the members home. Whilst I was waiting two men passed me. They came up the street as from Wellgate. The light from a lamp was close at hand and the club windows enabled me to get a good view of the men. My attention was drawn to them because of an expression made by one which was 'we'll make the ------- pay for it'. Both appeared to be worse for drink as they went forward up the High Street. Shortly afterwards the two persons I was waiting for came out of the club and I drove them to West House. On my way I saw the two men and when I pulled up, I again saw them going in the direction of Canklow. After they had passed I was taken into the house and had a glass of spirits given to me. Mr Wilfred Hurst spoke to the men. Something was said about what they were doing out of bed and they replied and the matter passed over. I was perfectly sober. To the best of my knowledge it would be 11.40 pm when the men passed me in the High Street. One of the men was carrying a small walking stick. On the Friday following I went to the Workhouse and saw a dead body. That was the body of one of the men I saw in the street on the Wednesday night. On Saturday last the 28th ult., I went to the police office. I saw a number of men in the yard; there would be a dozen or more. Among these dozen men, I saw the other man I saw in the street that night. I picked him out and that man is the prisoner - the man who also carried the stick to which I have referred'.

Holmes was closely cross examined on which of the two men had made the remark about being the ones to 'pay for it' but he could not say for sure. He also stated that he did not knew either man before that night. He had also been asked to pick out David Coe in an identity parade, but he stated that he was not one of the two men. Mr Netherwood Bentley of West House, Rotherham gave evidence which concurred with the cab mans statement. At this point the Mayor adjourned the inquest until 10 am the following morning, as it was said that there were still eight more witnesses for the prosecution to examine.

44

Chapter Seven: Magistrates Court. The Second Day.

The following day Wood was again brought before the magistrates and once again the court was packed with local people anxious to see the outcome. The first witness was Henry Dawes the publican of the Stag Inn at Herringthorpe, Rotherham. He told the bench:

'I remember the prisoner coming in to my house between eight o'clock and quarter past on the morning of the 19 February. He was supplied with a pint of beer and ginger beer and afterwards was supplied with another pint and bread and cheese. He was then supplied with more to drink and he took the money from his trousers pocket, from which he brought a handful of silver and copper, mixed together. He told me he had been at Rotherham the night before, and had got so drunk that he could not get to Whiston and had stopped all night in a shed in one of Mr Leedham's grass fields. Charles Roberts, quarry master came to my house that morning about nine o'clock, and sat in the same room as the prisoner. I noticed during the day that the prisoner was wearing a watch, having a bright steel curb chain, with a seal at the end. On one occasion near eleven o'clock when I was out of the room in which the prisoner was, I heard of the murder. Having heard of it I went into the room where Roberts and the prisoner were, and told them that I heard that a murder had been committed near to Canklow Wood. I did not know then who the man was that had been murdered. The prisoner made no remark whatever on the subject at that time. Charles Young alias Mills entered and joined the other men and I asked him if he had heard anything about the murder. He replied that he had heard the murder spoken of, but not who the murdered man was. Mills and Wood then had a conversation on their experiences at Wakefield and then Wood asked Mills if he knew if he knew a man with one arm that lived at Catcliffe. Mills mentioned the name of a letter carrier, but Wood said it was not the person he referred to. Wood left my house about three o'clock. I saw Wood handling the watch chain, and the seal which was appended to it had something like a blood stone in it which was affixed in some sort of bow'.

Henry Dawes stated that Wood made no attempt to hide the watch and that he knew Wood previously as he had been in his house before. On that occasion he left with another man who was not known to the landlord. When cross examined he also confirmed that there was shed in Mr Leedham's field.

Charles Roberts was the next to give his evidence and he too commented how he had seen the prisoner handling the watch and trying to move the hands with his fingers. He asked if it worked properly and Wood told him that it worked well enough. He then told Roberts a complete fabrication of how his father, himself and brother Jim all decided to buy six guinea watches from Mr Needham one day. His father paid for his watch in cash, but that he and his brother paid weekly or monthly for theirs. It was noted that throughout Roberts statements about the watch, that the prisoner appeared agitated and flushed. Roberts also spoke about Wood telling him that he got drunk the night before and that he had left Rotherham about 11.30 pm. He recounted how he had spent the night in Mr Leedham's shed, which had no straw just 'chop' or chaff to sleep on. He described the clothes that Wood had been wearing at the time as being grey trousers with patches on the knees and that the patches seemed to be put on underneath with the cloth sewn over them. The waistcoat was in the same material and the overcoat he had seen at the police office, was the same as he had been wearing at the time. When he saw him the next day, Roberts stated that the prisoner was not wearing the same trousers, which were of a darker colour and made of fustian or moleskin.

Charles Young alias Mills then gave his evidence of going to the Stag on the morning of the 18 February. He said:

'In the taproom I found the last witness, Mr Dawes and the prisoner. In reply to Dawes I said I had heard that a man had been murdered, from Mr Jenkins Carter, who said he had seen a policeman with a hedge stake. I did not know the murdered man's name. In reply to the prisoner I said I knew a man at Brinsworth that had a hook on his arm, whose name is Cliffe and he is a letter carrier. Wood said "I don't mean that letter carrier". I said I didn't know any other man from that place with a hook on his arm, and the prisoner said "well he is some relation to that man". I said its a

very bad job and they'll make someone sit up for it. Wood immediately volunteered the statement that he had been out all night. I said "it was a grand night to be out. I expect thou wor under cover somewhere Jack". He said "No I wornt I stayed in t'field" I said "thou wont tell me that is false. No man could sleep out as it rained and blew". He said "I wor very drunk" I said "I should say thou were wor drunk if thou laid out"'.

Young then noted a chain which Wood sported on his waistcoat and told him 'thous doing better than me, Jack if thou can sport a watch'. To this the prisoner merely smiled. Cross examined the witness stated that he hadn't actually seen the watch, just the chain hanging down from his pocket on the left hand side of his waistcoat. To another juror he stated that he had known Wood for years, but had never seen him wear a watch before. One of the magistrates enquired about his former life to which Young replied 'I have been in trouble for nearly everything but murder' to which there was laughter in the court with which Wood joined in.

Robert Poynter from Roydsmoor near Whiston next gave evidence of the meeting with Wood and gaining possession of the watch whose hands were stuck on either ten minutes before, or ten minutes past two o'clock. The watch, which he managed to start again, was in his possession from Thursday afternoon until Saturday morning. He said that the following day he was in Rotherham where he saw an account of the murder and that a watch was missing. The next morning he took the watch back to Wood at his fathers house. He arrived between 7 and 8 o'clock in the morning, but no one was up. Poyter then said:

'I knocked, and his father came down. Before that I heard someone call "hey up". It was the prisoner who called out. I went in and while I was speaking to the prisoner's father, the prisoner came down into the room. I asked the father whether Jack was in and said "I have brought him this watch back". The prisoner stepped forward and said "Did you think it was his watch Bob" I said I didn't know what to think. Before I left the prisoner said I was not to say anything about it. I went away leaving the watch with the prisoner'.

A carter Francis Ellis who was employed by Mr Moorhouse and lived at Bole Hill, Treeton near Rotherham was the next witness. He stated that he had met Wood on Thursday afternoon [the day after the murder] at about 5.40 pm he was going down Wellgate when Wood suggested that they go for a drink. Ellis told him that he had no money, to which Wood replied 'I have plenty. I have spent plenty and have plenty left in my pocket'. Then:

'we went to the Three Tuns Inn, a little lower down the road, and we had a pint of beer in the passage. Wood both ordered the pint [in a jug] and paid for it. Wood poured me out a glass of beer from the jug he held in his hand. I handed the glass to him and said "Sup yourself first John". I then asked if he had heard tell of the murder on Canklow and he said "no". He asked me what the name of the dead man was, and I replied that I thought it was Coe. Wood then began to tremble, and said "take the glass and the pitcher Frank" and I took it away from him. He began to shed tears, said it was sorry it was poor Coe, as he was with him the previous night at eleven o'clock. On leaving the public house, I gave Wood a ride as far as the top of Mansfield Road. We there saw another man called Fred Grey. Wood shouted Fred to him and Grey asked what he wanted. He said "come I want thee". I then left them together'.

Fred Grey corroborated the evidence of the previous witness before relating how Wood had told him the same alibi that he had been with Coe, left him at 11 pm and had slept out the previous night. Then he said:

'When we got to the Belvedere Inn we went in and had four pints of beer between us, and a cigar each, which John Wood paid for. He took the money, silver and copper mixed from his trousers pocket. I remember Mr Hill the landlord coming into the room and a police officer was with him. Hill and Wood had a conversation as to where Wood and John Coe had been the night before. When we went on the way to Whiston, we met Hill again and he and Wood had another conversation'.

William Thornton the constable stated that he had gone to the Belvedere where the prisoner had admitted that he was with the dead man on the night of the murder. Wood then started to get aggressive when the constable told him he would make a good witness and give the police some information. Wood said to him *'----you, you are getting onto me. I know nothing about the ----fellow'*. The constable then told the court that he had called at the prisoners house that night again. He stated that *'I had some conversation with him; he ordered me out of the house, and I left'*. Another constable John Bonnett from Whiston then gave evidence of the statement made by Wood at his parents house on 19 February where again he contradicted himself about David Coe. At first the prisoner had said that he and Wood left David at Oakwood Park, Moorgate before going into the Belvedere and the Butchers Arms. Then he read out the prisoner statement. Wood told him:

'When we came out Jack Coe, this man they say is killed, asked me if I could tell him where we could find and ----- [some prostitutes] *I said I could, and we went into a public house in Wellgate, where we had some beer. We found that it wasn't the place we wanted to be at, so we went to another pub and had some beer there. This man they say is killed paid for a gallon of beer, which was put into one of those basket bottles. We all went out together there to the bottom of Old Hill, and Jack and David Coe went up the Old Hill, but I would not go with them. They left me at the bottom of Old Hill about half past eleven o'clock'.*

Cross examined about whether constable Bonnett was sure that the prisoner had said that David Coe was there, he stated that was what Wood had said, despite the fact that he had previously told him they had left David Coe at Oakwood Park. After making this statement, Wood then turned to his mother and asked her what time it would have been when he got home the previous night. She replied 'thou never came home last night Jack. I wont tell a lie for thee. I never saw thee after seven o'clock'. His father confirmed his wife's statement, before Wood gave a rambling statement about seeing a man following him who he thought was detective. Bonnett said that he had then taken Wood to see the Superintendent about 11.35 pm. When he seemed reluctant to go, Bonnett took him into custody. Superintendent John Gillett

50

followed his colleague onto the witness stand and described taking the prisoners statement that night, which was basically the same as he had told before. However he admitted that he had not cautioned the prisoner before taking his statement, as David Coe was already in police custody and the Superintendent had no reason to doubt Woods guilt. He admitted:

'at the time I had no reason for doubting that David Coe was the man who ought to be in custody. I made use of no threat or promise to Wood when I asked him for the information which he gave me in that statement'.

Cross examined by one of the magistrates Superintendent Gillett stated that Wood appeared sober, although he may have previously been drinking.

Witness Robert Rotherham a joiner from Whiston then gave evidence of seeing Wood on the morning of the 19th at just after seven o'clock, but that he was not coming from the direction of Leedham's farm. He was about a mile away from the Stag and heading in that direction. A farm labourer Richard Rimmington told the magistrates that he had met Wood near Whiston Common and the prisoner had begged him for something to eat. He gave him some bread and cheese before asking him if he had done the murder, to which Wood replied that he hadn't. Rimmington admitted that at that time he had not known that the police were looking for the prisoner.

Sergeant Martin Sykes of Laughton then gave evidence of apprehending Wood on the road leading from Woodsetts to Worksop. He described how he was in plain clothes when he saw a group of four men coming towards him. He told the magistrates:

'my attention was drawn to one of the four who was walking with his head down as if to conceal his face, he was slouching with his hands in his pockets. As the men got closer to the horses head, I saw that one of the men was a man I knew, Samuel Pond. I called out to him "Sam who have you got with you?". He replied "I don't know he is a stranger". The man who was then crouching looked sideways at the pony and trap and I jumped out and collared him. I

did not know then who he was. I asked him "what are you doing here?". He said "I am looking for a job". I said "Where do you come from?". He said "from Worksop" I took off his hat and saw a scar on his head I said "Is your name Wood?" He said "yes" and I told him "your the man I'm looking for".

When he was charged at Laughton police station with the theft of the silver watch Wood had stated 'I never had the watch in my life and those who say so are liars'. Again on the way back to Rotherham the prisoner, perhaps realising the amount of trouble he was in, repeated to the sergeant:

'they say I had a watch at the Stag. I never had a watch. Why should I give it Moody's man [Robert Poynter] *for. I never killed the man. I never saw Moody's man for three weeks or a month when I saw him pass our house going from Whiston to Rotherham. I left Jack Coe at the bottom of Old Hill, Wellgate at half-past eleven that night'.*

James Gooderick Needham gave evidence that he had sold the silver watch to Mrs Ann Coe, the mother of the deceased man and he had seen it several times in John Coe's possession. He had repaired it several times and the last time he had seen it was 13 December 1878. He stated:

'I know the prisoners father, to whom I have sold a silver watch. That was on 16 February 1877 and the price was £5.5s., which was paid for by instalments. There was no makers name on that watch. In fourteen days afterwards I sold a silver lever watch to the prisoners brother, at the same price, which also had no makers name on it. All my sales of watches are booked, whether they are cash or credit. I have never sold a watch to, or mended one for the prisoner, nor is there any entry in my books of any such sale'.

However it was the last surprise witness to give the final evidence that sealed Wood's fate. He was John Riggs a file grinder who said he had been locked up for being drunk in Rotherham on the night of 28 February. The following morning about 8 am, having sobered up, he went to Woods cell and the men had a conversation through a closed door. After Woods asked Riggs what was the latest in the press about 'this job' Riggs told him that 'the watch will do for you'. Woods replied that 'if that's all that turned up against me, it will only be two or three months for manslaughter'. Riggs told him 'It will be Marwood [the executioner] and the rope for you', to which the prisoner just smiled. Riggs then told the court that he had been released from the cells later that morning. However the previous night he had been in College Yard when two police officers asked him about the conversation he had with Wood when he had been in the cells, and he told them. When he was cross examined on why he hadn't told the police at the time, he told the court that he didn't think they would believe his evidence because he was a prisoner. As this man was giving his evidence, It was noticeable that Woods face became flushed and the veins stood out prominently on his forehead. As the man continued speaking, he stared at the witness with great intensity, and paid more attention to him than he had done to previous witnesses.

After hearing this damning statement Mr Parker Rhodes asked the Mayor to commit the prisoner to take his trial at the assizes. Consequently his defence solicitor Mr Clegg made up his mind to reserve his clients defence. He stated that:

'I cannot but think that there is quite enough evidence before you at any rate, to put the prisoner on his trial. Therefore I don't intend to inflict any remarks upon your Worships time and I don't propose to do so by making any observations on the subject'.

The Mayor asked Wood if he had anything to say in his defence, and he replied 'I am not guilty Sir', before he was sentenced to take his trial at the Yorkshire Spring Assizes and he was then removed back into the police cells.

Chapter Eight: The Trial and the Prosecutions Case.

On Wednesday 21 April 1880, prior to the commencement of the trial, the case of John Henry Wood was discussed between the judge, Justice Fitzjames Stephens and the Grand Jury for the Assizes at York. It was usual that before the assizes started, that they would discussed any special cases which would be tried before them. The judge was concerned about the amount of circumstantial evidence that had been gathered in Woods case. This boiled down to both accused and victim having been seen in each others company before the murder, and the fact that the prisoner, Wood had not returned home that night. Justice Stephens told the Grand Jury that the one important factor in the case was that, after the murder the prisoner had possession of the watch which the dead man had with him when he was murdered. The next day the prisoner had been seen with the watch, when he had never been seen with any watch before. The fact that it had belonged to the deceased could not be argued, due to the peculiarities of the marks on the watch which were consistent with this practice. The judge commented on the fact that Wood constant playing with the watch 'reminded one of a boy who had become possessed of a new plaything' he consulted it so often. He concluded that the one fact the Grand Jury could not dispute was that the prisoner was with the murdered man up to the last moment, and that soon after his death he was found in possession of his property. He urged them to return a true bill against the prisoner in order that he may take his trial. Shortly after 5 pm a true bill was found against John Henry Wood of the murder of John Coe, and it was announced that the trial was to take place on Friday 23 April at 10.30 am.

When Wood was brought into court in front of Mr Justice Stephens at the Yorkshire Spring Assizes at York, it was noticeable that, although he was still wearing the same clothes as he had at the magistrates hearing, his appearance had been much improved. The prisoner had now had grown a fine smooth moustache and his cheeks were adorned with mutton chop whiskers. When asked if he had anything to say to the charge, Wood said in a clear voice 'not

54

guilty my lord' and he was given a seat. Throughout the trial reporters noted that Wood paid strict attention to the evidence laid out before him in a calm and lucid manner, almost as if a recital of the awful tragedy had nothing whatsoever to do with him. Mr Lawrence Gane, who had been instructed by Mr Clegg and Sons of Sheffield, had been appointed as his defence counsel. Mr Lockwood, the prosecution opened the case by outlining the case and in a speech which lasted over an hour, went over in great detail the events of the night of the murder. He described the murder scene as being committed 'in a lonely part of the town, about 300 yards from any dwelling place of any description'. Relating the events of the night he concluding by stating to the jury:

'It is no part of my duty to do any more at present than to state the evidence to you, and if calmly and considerately weighing that evidence, you should come to the conclusion that it all points to the prisoner being guilty of murder, then you know perfectly well what your verdict must be'.

Then the witnesses repeated their evidence, which was the same as they had given before, with perhaps more emphasis on the silver watch. Joseph Hawksworth described finding the body, but when cross examined, now he could not say with any certainty whether John Coe was still alive when he first came upon him. Other witnesses gave the same evidence that they had at the magistrates court, before the victims mother, Mrs Anne Coe took the stand. She stated that her son had about £2 on him when he left on the day of the murder, and also that he had not been with her when she bought the watch at Mr Needham's shop. Her husband gave evidence of taking the watch back to Needham's to be repaired, and he remembered the watchmaker pointing out the damage made by the knife when trying to open the back section. There were some witnesses however who had not appeared before the Rotherham magistrates, whose evidence, nevertheless all pointed to Woods guilt. Thomas Cliffe of Brinsworth stated that he was the deceased mans uncle and indicated how he had only one arm with a hook at the end of it. In order to contradict Wood stating that he did not know him, he told the judge that he knew Wood before the murder and Wood knew him. However he stated that he was not a letter carrier, but a labourer. A woman, Caroline Oates, the wife of the landlord of the Butchers Arms related how the prisoner and the deceased visited her house about 9pm on the night of the murder. She then said that she saw the prisoner again two days later, after he had been taken to give his statement to Superintendent Gillett. He told her:

'you see I have soon got at liberty: they said I was not the man they wanted. The idea of me robbing a man of his watch and money! I have got a watch and money of my own'.

Thomas Wright a puddler of Rotherham stated that he was in the Pack Horse Inn on the Wednesday night after the murder and saw Wood and a man he didn't know come in. Drinks were brought for them which Wood paid for, and he remembered the stranger taking out a watch and saying that it was half past nine. He noted the man complain 'I've a good mind to chop half this chain off; its too long'. The next witness was Elizabeth Saunders of Wellgate Rotherham, who also swore that the deceased man had a peeled stick in his possession when he was at her house. She told the court that he tapped his boot with it, and on one occasion had let it fall to the ground. Her companion, Annie Wilkes picked it up and asked for it for her son, but the deceased man only laughed in reply.

Another witness, Frederick Wadsworth living at Herringthorpe said he was out with his father's horses about 8 am on the 19 February. He saw the prisoner who asked him if he had the time and Wadsworth told him that he did not have a watch. Then the prisoner pulled out a silver watch on a steel chain from his waistcoat pocket, and indicated that his watch had stopped. The witness told the judge that he knew the shed in Mr Leedham's field, but the prisoner was not coming from that direction when he saw him that morning. Charles Roberts a quarry owner also gave evidence of seeing the prisoner with the watch the day after the murder. Charles Young stated that on the morning of 19 February he had been hawking at a house in Herringthorpe when he heard from a man employed as a carter, that he had seen a policeman with a hedgestake at Canklow and heard that a body had been found. He had been told that the victim was a relation of a man named Cliffe, who had a hook instead of a hand and was a letter carrier. At that point when cross examined about his evidence

Young claimed that he had known Wood for eight or ten years and had never seen him in possession of a watch before. The prisoner had told him that he had slept all night in a field which Young questioned, and he too commented that at the time Wood was playing with the watch. Young had said to him 'thou's doing better then me Jack if thou can sport a watch', but Wood just smiled. When cross-examined the witness claimed that he did not actually see the watch, but he had seen the chain which hung straight down from a pocket on the left side of his waistcoat.

Francis Ellis repeated his evidence of how upset Wood had been when he heard that the man who had been murdered was John Coe. Police Constable Thornton of Rotherham Police gave evidence of interviewing the prisoner at the Belvedere Inn on Thursday night. When he adding that Wood might make a good witness, the prisoner swore at him and said the officer was 'getting onto him and he knew nothing about the bloody fellow'. When he afterwards went to Woods house the prisoner told him 'I've seen you before at the Belvedere Inn. You know what I told you there, and I shall tell you no more'. The officer stated that at this point the prisoner became excited and his parents requested that he leave to which he complied with their wishes. Police Constable Bennett said that he had taken a statement from Wood at his fathers house, and when he asked him what time he had returned home the previous night, his parents denied that he had been at home at all. The prisoner had then said to the witness crucially:

'I could tell thee something that would make a bloody good thing for thee, but not before these bastards, they are not to be trusted. I will tell thee in the morning'

Wood then admitted that he had slept in the shed at Broom. PC Thornton then gave evidence about taking the prisoner before Mr Gillett to be interviewed. He was cross examined as to whether the Superintendent had cautioned the prisoner before he made his statement. Bennett told him that he hadn't, because at the time he did not consider the prisoner to be guilty. Mr Justice Stephens interrupted to remark that he did not think it necessary that a policeman should caution a man, if the man felt inclined to make a statement. Superintendent John Gillett followed his colleague onto the stand and he too gave evidence about the statement made by the prisoner. He said at the time he had David Coe in custody on a charge of wilful murder, and he only wanted Wood to tell him what he knew about the matter. Police Sergeant Martin Sykes described the capture of Wood and the fact that when he was arrested at Rotherham and charged with murder and stealing a watch, Wood claimed 'I never had a watch in my life'.

Mr Needham repeated his statement that he had never sold a watch to the prisoner, although he had sold lever watches to both Wood's father and brother and they had both paid for the watches in instalments. Mrs Needham corroborated his evidence and said that she had looked through the shop book, but she could not find any entry of a sale of a watch to the prisoner. John Riggs gave his evidence which was corroborated by another man, Thomas Burton of the Crofts, Rotherham, who had also been in the cells. At this point the judge interrupted and stated that he attached little importance to prisoners gossip in the cells. Mr Lockwood then summed up the case for the prosecution. He told the jury:

'The object of the prosecution was not to strive for a conviction, but to establish the truth. In my humble judgement the witnesses have given their evidence not for the purpose of bringing guilt home to the prisoner, but they had corroborated to the full, the statement he was instructed to make'.

He then reviewed the evidence and touched upon the salient points of the case, and concluded by referring the jury to the nature of the duty they were required to perform. By this time it was 5.55 pm and so it was agreed that the proceedings would best be adjourned until 9 am the following morning when Mr Gane would make his speech for the defence, the verdict of the jury will be given and his lordship will sum up the case. At this point Wood was the removed from the dock and taken down to the cells.

Chapter Nine: The Defence and the Judges Summing Up.

On Saturday 24 April 1880 Wood was brought back into the assizes to hear his defence counsel make a speech on his behalf, which lasted two and a quarter hours. Mr Gane began by thanking the judge for leaving his speech until today, after hearing all the evidence which had taken so long. He said that he had not cross examined too many of the witnesses, for the simple reason that much of the evidence pointed to the prisoners guilt. However, what could not be denied is that much of the evidence was circumstantial against his client. He asked the jury to think about the consequences for the prisoner and the 'tremendous results of any mistakes they might make in their decision of the case'. Mr Gane then pointed to the three major issues which argued his clients case. He said that three of the witnesses had clearly stated that the prisoner and the victim were not enemies with no previous quarrel. Wood did not force his company on the deceased man, and according to witnesses, at least two of the drinks had been bought by him. Mr Gane spoke about the stick which witnesses had said had undoubtedly been in the possession of Wood before the murder, and questioned whether he would have left it behind, if he truly intended to murder the dead man. What could be more natural than he gave the stick back to Coe as they parted, and that Coe had taken it to the murder scene at Canklow. If Wood had indeed been guilty of the murder, why would he leave evidence of his guilt at the scene of the crime? If he had left the scene, and then remembered having forgotten the stick, there was ample time to go back and retrieve it in the still hours of the night.

The defence then came to the missing watch, which he claimed was the most compelling part of the evidence for the prosecution. Yet the watch itself was not unusual in anyway, and he surmised that a hundred similar ones could be found in Rotherham or York that very day. The victims father had mentioned a crack in the dial of the watch, but the maker, Mr Needham could not recall such a blemish. The marks on the dome of the watch made by prising open the case was exceedingly common, and could not be used as a specific identity of the watch. Therefore it should not be used as evidence to say that a man was guilty of murder because he had such a watch in his possession. Mr Gane would state that nothing was unusual about the watch, chain or seal, and articles of the same description might well be in the possession of the prisoner as well as the deceased man at the same time. The jeweller, Mr Needham had admitted that he had sold a lever watch to the prisoners father and brother, but the defence claimed that the watch, being only a cheap one, might not have been entered in Mr Needhams books for that very reason. If Wood had committed the murder, he asked the jury, 'would any murderer he be so imbecilic as to play with the watch openly in the company of others?' Why should the prisoner, having supposedly murdered a man for his money and the watch, then go about within a short distance of the site of the murder, showing the watch about and bringing it to the notice of others. The defence claimed that no man would murder another he had known for some time, and been with for most of the day as witnessed by several people, for the sake of a watch and a paltry sum of money. If that was the prisoners intention, he could have attacked him and robbed him at several points throughout the day whilst they were both drinking. There were suspicions that Wood had gone on the run which pointed to his clear guilt, but the defence pointed out that when he had been told by Mr Gillett to attend the inquest, he had done so. He only decided to flee once he thought the police's evidence against him was overwhelming. Therefore it was not surprising that was slouching and he held his head down when he was finally arrested by Sergeant Sykes. Alone, without friends and in complete despair he had done the only thing that a suspected man in his position might have done. At this point in Mr Gane's speech, matters were interrupted by the prisoner in the dock falling into a fit calling on mercy from God. Wood cried:

'Oh my God, my father, my heavenly father. Oh my God, God remember me. Oh God have mercy on me; spare me; be with me my God. Oh, oh'.

He was laid on his back by warders with him in the dock before the governor of York prison, Captain Twyford shouted at them to hold his head up. He then gave the prisoner a drink of brandy and water, which he had in his possession. Dr Hardwicke of Rotherham also attended to Wood, before he was joined by the prison surgeon, Mr

Anderson. The judge suggested that the prisoner should be taken out of the courtroom for a while, and he was taken out into the yard for some fresh air. About ten minutes later he had fully recovered so that when the judge asked him if he wanted to adjourn the trial, Wood told him that he wanted to proceed with the case. At this point the prisoner was given a chair to sit on and the trial continued. As Mr Gane continued with his defence, some deep sighs were heard coming from the prisoner, who had a warder on each side of him.

Mr Gane stated that he did not intend to keep the court much longer and then referred to the fact that Wood told some of the 'flattest' lies that any man in his despair at being charged with murder, could fabricate. He asked the jury 'did that alone not show the nature of the mans honesty?' Any man in the same position would say anything that came to him, yet when he was finally charged the prisoner stuck to the same story. As to the cabman Holmes' evidence, without doubting the mans honesty, how could he say that the two men he had seen in the High Street, were the same two men he had seen at West House. They were across the road from him and there was no bright light shining, as it had earlier from the Gentlemen's Club on the High Street. The defence then went to what he claimed was the greatest mystery of this case which had arisen:

'at the house of "Big Liz" on Old Hill. The two men had no quarrel there but they went away in an extraordinary manner. They left without an apparent reason, and neither saying "good night" or speaking about returning. They left behind in the house a man named Charles Staunton, who did not live there and whose whereabouts since, no light has been thrown. It was a striking thing that Coe and Wood, going up High Street should talk about "making the ---- pay for it" if nothing had occurred'.

He then stated that the hedge stick which had been the murder weapon had never been seen in the possession of the prisoner, and that in fact there was no evidence to connect him with the weapon. He spoke of the amount of blood found at the scene and the fact that the deceased man had been struck on the front of his head. He asked the jury 'would not the man who committed the murder have much blood on his clothes?'. Driving the point home, he said there was not sufficient blood on Woods apparel to warrant them in supposing that he had struck the blows. Mr Gane urged the jury to remember those small discrepancies when they assess the prosecutions case against the prisoner. Finally he stated that if the jury had any shadow of doubt on any of the evidence, they were to give the prisoner the benefit of that doubt and give a not guilty verdict. The speech, which lasted two and a quarter hours concluded that 'it was as much the jury's part to protect the innocence as to perform their duty to society, and the former was the highest duty of the two'

At this point Mr Gane told the judge that he did not intend to call any witnesses. Mr Lockwood, the prosecution then told the court:

'the object of the prosecution was not to strive for a conviction, but to establish the truth. In my humble judgement the witnesses had given their evidence, not for the purpose of bringing guilt home to the prisoner, but they had corroborated to the full the statement he was instructed to make'

The judge then began his summing up at 11.25 am which occupied the court for the next two and a half hours. As part of his speech he mentioned 'Big Liz' and the 'horrible life she was leading' to which there was some tittering in the gallery. The judge warned those persons in the gallery that 'if he heard any levity of that kind, in a case of this seriousness, he would have the court cleared'. Mr Justice Stephens said that it did not follow that because Wood went along the way home with Coe that he intended to waylay and murder him. He might, as any drunken fellow would with another, go on the way home without any particular motive. However there was no doubting the fact that murder had been committed.

'because if a man beat another about the head furiously and vehemently and fractured it in three pieces, if that were not murder, I do not know what it could be'.

Therefore he could not suggest that the victim had been murdered for anything else other than the sake of his watch and money. He pointed out that there were a lot of wicked people in the world who would kill for a paltry amount of money, as unhappily his own experience in courtrooms proved, and this was particularly true once drink was involved. He also reminded the jury that although the man had been killed in a very violent way, there was very little blood found on the prisoner himself. There were fifty ways in which a person might get blood upon his clothes, and what ever that fact was worth, it was something in the prisoners favour.

Referring to the peeled stick and hedgestake found at the scene of the crime, the judge observed that many persons who committed murder, constantly overlooked such things as leaving the weapon at the scene. However he had an observation he had to make regarding the peeled stick being left in the field. Justice Stevens said that whoever struck the blows with the stake would be compelled to hold it with both hands to wield it with full effect, and to do that the smaller stick must have been dropped. Their minds were so disturbed by the terrible actions they had taken, that leaving the stick behind was one of the ways which may incriminate them. It is possible that the prisoner by getting possession of the watch, could not turn his attention away from it to anything else. He concurred with Mr Gane's opinion that Wood had openly played with the watch, unable to help himself 'like that of a boy with a new watch playing with it for the first time'. Mr Gane had also stated that if the watch had been the motive for the robbery that Wood would not have exhibited it in the mad way in which he did. The defence had also asserted that the watch was of a common make which could be found anywhere. However, as the judge pointed out, the watch answering that description in every particular had been taken from the murdered man, and that had been the crucial point of the matter.

Mr Justice Stephen then came to the crux of the matter saying that the jury should ask themselves where that watch was now? Whilst defending every word the learned counsel for the defence had spoken, he told the jury that to remember that if the watch had in reality belonged to Wood, why had it not been produced in court? Mr Justice Stephens said that the jury had to take into account everything they had heard in court and it was now up to them to decide the prisoners fate. The jury left the room at 1.50 pm to consider their verdict, and once the jury had retired, Wood was also removed from the dock. However the wait for the prisoner was very short, the jury returning after only twenty minutes to find John Henry Wood guilty of the murder of John Coe. The judge asked Wood if he had anything to say in his defence. In reply the prisoner said 'Sir I am not guilty, I have not done the crime that I am now convicted for. I am truly innocent'. The clerk then ordered 'silence in the court' before the judge put on the black cap and passed the sentence of death on Wood. He told him:

'You stand convicted of wilful murder committed under circumstances of extreme atrocity. The jury have patiently heard the whole of the evidence. They have carefully listened to the arguments of your counsel, and they feel no doubt that you are guilty of the crime of which you have been charged. Neither do I feel any doubt that you are guilty of the crime. You passed the day with your victim in what you regarded as pleasure and good fellowship. You went with him from place to place as his companion and friend. You followed him from haunts of intemperance and haunts of vice, to a place where you thought you could effect your purpose without discovery. You drew him, how we know not, into the neighbourhood of the stack where his body was found. You seized the murderous weapon and you struck him to death with repeated blows, and you did so for the wretched and paltry object of robbing him of a few shillings and a watch and chain. For that crime you must die'.

He then passed the sentence of death as he told him:

'You, John Henry Wood shall be taken to the place from whence you came, and from thence to a place of execution and there you be hanged by the neck until you are dead, and that your body be afterwards buried within the precincts of the prison in which you shall have been last confined after your sentence. And may the Lord have mercy on your soul'.

The prisoner was about to be removed from the court by the wardens when he spoke again. He said without hesitation 'Thank you sir, I did not know where the stack was. I had been away at the same time. I do not know anything about the stack'. He was then removed and the court rose.

Naturally all the newspapers, both national and local avidly took up the reporting of the trial and for many days after Wood had been convicted, the matter was discussed at great length in the town. It was reported that when the news arrived at Rotherham that Wood had been sentenced to death, it was thought by many people to be a forgone conclusion and little surprise was shown at the verdict. It was said that when the hedge stake was produced in court, many of the spectators at the back of the court had risen to their feet to get a better view of the terrible weapon, but Wood remained seated and quiet. The only sign of animation he showed was when he consulted with Mr W E Clegg, the solicitor for the defence in order to challenge some of the witnesses statements. One reporter from the *Sheffield and Rotherham Independent* stated that Woods very demeanour was totally different to that in the magistrates court where at some statements made in the proceedings 'his eyes almost stood out of their sockets, and the veins of his forehead at times became very prominent'. However during the trial the prisoner had appeared quite unruffled. Indeed this may have been because every courtesy had been offered to Wood for his comfort during the time he was in court. The courtesy of the court officials had spread the trial out over two days, ensuring that all the evidence could be better heard, in order that it would not be too demanding for both the jury and the prisoner. It also mentioned that on the second day the judge promptly took his chair at exactly 9 am, an hour earlier than when cases usually began at the assizes. The report stated that Mr Gane had impressed the jury with the earnestness of his speech and made some very valid points on the prisoners behalf. After having retained his composure, it was only when Mr Gane alluded to the fact that on the day of his capture, when he described him as a man bereft of companions, believed by none and brought to the depth of despair, did the prisoner swoon. As Mr Gane continued with his eloquent defence of the prisoner Wood was heard to give several deep sighs. When the jury returned after only 20 minutes consultation it seemed to many in the court that they were unanimous in their verdict. Woods scanning of their faces must have concluded their verdict and therefore he received it calmly and quietly. This was wondrous considering his previously hysterical outbreak, and therefore many felt that he must have been guilty or else why did he cry out for mercy 'unless he had the fear of death upon him'.

After several days of rehashing the trial over and over, the reporters were expecting a confession. They came to the conclusion that:

'Woods assertion have led some to almost doubt his criminality; but if he be guilty, he certainly would not be the first murderer who, having had the sentence of death passed upon him, has pleaded that he was innocent, and still before the dread sentence was carried out, has confessed the crime laid to his charge'.

Another newspaper the *Leeds Mercury* mentioned that when the judge assumed the black cap, the prisoner, as was the custom, rose to his feet and for the first time many of the reporters saw him fully. At that point it was noted that his shoulders were very broad, more than had been assumed from his somewhat feminine facial features. Wood had listened to the sentence of death with 'a wonderful composure' before he thanked the judge, whilst remarking that he did not know the spot on which the body had been found. It was this final assertion that led some local people to doubt his guilt and the reporter ended 'the greatest interest will be paid as to whether or not he makes a final confession'. A week later on 1 May it was announced that John Henry Wood would be hanged for the murder of John Coe on Tuesday 11 May 1880 within the walls of York Castle prison.

Chapter Ten: The Condemned Man

If the people of Rotherham were disturbed at the murder, the people of Whiston were stunned at what had happened to one of their own. Although Wood had a criminal history, he was well liked in the village. In his early years had regularly attended the Parish Church Sunday School at the Wesleyan Chapel, which was situated just a few yards from his parents home. He was said to have been be a hard working man, a very pleasant fellow labourer, a boon companion and one who 'in his cups' was not closed fisted with his money. At that time the village of Whiston was described as a very rural area with a small population. On the 7 May 1880 a description was printed in the *Sheffield and Rotherham Independent* which stated that:

'The village stands back from the main road, its seclusiveness lending it a peculiar charm. A portion of it lies ensconced in a small valley, the sides of which rise to a considerable height, and from the greatest altitude the parish church dominates the hamlet. The valley is watered with dams here and there giving change to its ordinary current, dotted at intervals by ducks which dabble delightedly in the stream. Wooden bridges cross the rivulet and flights of steps lead up to the series of terraces which abound, and where dwellings, whitewashed and red roofed are perched'.

The house of the condemned man was also described. It was said to be 'an old fashioned dwelling which stands back a little beyond a batch of other cottages, fringing the roadside leading from Whiston to Royds Moor. Here it was that a reporter had called the day before, and Woods father aged 70 showed him a letter he had just received from his son. It was the usual kind of letter from a man facing death and read:

My Dear Father and Mother, Brothers and Sisters,
I have seen my sister today and brother-in-law and want my brothers to take a warning from me and never go to the Chakers [Chequers] again. Because they will speak evil of you, as they did by me. You must go to some place of worship and then you will never get into bad company. If you do so you will gain Heaven at

last. *Dear Allan James Wood,* [his brother] *Dear Father and Mother and the whole of you, I should like to see as many that can come, so no more at present. God bless you all. Goodbye From your affect. son*
JOHN H WOOD

Unlike the prolific stories of the crime which had circulated in Whiston and Rotherham, there was a great secrecy around the condition of Wood as he lay within the condemned cell. When local reporters tried to elicit any information from the governor, Captain Twyford or the chaplain, Rev. A W Baldwin, they would only reply 'I will say nothing'. However they did manage to winkle out a description of the condemned cell at the prison at York. It was said to be quite spacious, but having no natural light, made it a very gloomy apartment. Immediately adjoining the small room was another room in which will be placed a scaffold for the execution. Local reporters also established that Wood had not made any formal or written statement, which amounted to 'an admission of confession of his guilt'. As was usual in cases of execution, two warders were in constant attendance upon the condemned man, and the governor and chaplain visited him daily. It was also said that Wood was resigned to his fate and held out little hope that he will escape the hangman's noose. A last visit was arranged for his parents to say goodbye to their son on Saturday 8 May 1880. They were accompanied by his sister (Mrs Alfred Whiteley) his brother-in-law Allen, and a second brother and sister-in-law (Mrs and Mrs Charles Greaves) Once again it was reported that the relatives left their home in Whiston in time to have some dinner with friends in Rotherham, who were reported as being 'very sympathetic to their circumstances'. They then caught the Midland train for York, which left the Masbrough Station at 2.01 pm, and arrived at York at 3.15 pm where they made their way immediately to the Castle prison. They were directed to the condemned cell by Captain Twyford, who was reported to be an amiable gentleman, although he had been quite upset about the publication of the letter sent from their son in the local newspaper. When they arrived at his cell they found Deputy Governor Edward Triffit was already in attendance, although he sat at a table in a far corner in order to give the family as much privacy as possible. The prisoner was reported as 'looking somewhat better than their previous visit, and more prepared to face the hangman'. Wood renewed his denial of any involvement in the murder, and stated that he would not be making any different statement on the subject. He told his family that it was hard to die for a crime of which he was not guilty, before he began to cry. Later, after speaking to the family, the local newspaper reported that:

'the prisoner was not as tidy in his person as he had previously been, and looked somewhat aged. His cheeks were wan and pale, his hair had grown rather unkempt, and his unshaven face detracts from his ordinarily clean appearance'.

His mother, concerned at his wasted appearance asked him if he was sleeping well. Wood told that her that he was sleeping as best as he could under the circumstances, but hadn't eaten much. However he also told his parents that he had been very kindly treated by the warders and the prison authorities, 'who could not have shown him more kindness than if they were his own relatives'.

Wood told his family that he had been distressed that the Hon. and Rev. Canon Howard the Vicar of Whiston had travelled to York, but permission to see his former parishioner had been refused. This was because he had no order to visit from the Secretary of State. Wood said that he was sorry that the Canon had a wasted journey, as he would have been glad to see him. He had often listened attentively to prayers and sermons from the Canon when he was a young boy. The family started to discuss the trial, but the Deputy Governor requested that they confine their conversation to prayers, and urging their son to confess, rather than criticising the events that had taken place in court. Wood ignored him and talked about the statement he had made, that he had never seen the stack where the murder took place. It seems that the felony that Wood had committed a few months previously in Rotherham had resulted in a prison sentence, and upon his release he had not visited the town more than four times altogether. Even on those occasions, he had rarely walked along Canklow Road, which, as we have already seen, was not the most direct route to Whiston. As regards the chaff on his boots, he told his parents that he had been threshing for Mr J D Styring at Whiston on the day of the murder. He also said that he was very disappointed that no effort had been made to get a reprieve. As requested by the prison authorities, before his visitors left the prison, they asked him again to confess his guilt for the crime for which he had been sentenced. Wood merely told them that he was innocent of the murder, and remarked that the judge himself would ultimately be arraigned before the same tribunal that he was going to face in a few days. He asked to be remembered to all his friends at Whiston and hoped that those he might have had differences with, would forgive him. The visit had lasted about an hour and a half, but the parents through the columns of the newspapers complained that the prison authorities had cut short their visit with their son. The Governor stated at the time that had not been the case, although the warders may have given that impression as they were trying to divert them from grief at a very difficult meeting. In fact the ploy may have been partially successful as it was reported that there were no tearful scenes in the cell, which usually accompany such last visits. However, not unnaturally, as Wood's family passed through the Castle gates they appeared quite overwhelmed by grief, but they were quickly put into a cab which had been hired for them, and taken to a Temperance Hotel where they had tea. After tea they went to the York station and left for home on the 6.25 pm train which arrived at Masbrough Station at 7.39 pm, and from there they made the journey home to Whiston on foot.

The day before the execution, local newspaper were debating as to whether any reporters would be allowed inside the prison to view the hanging. Since 1868 hangings were now always carried out behind prison walls, and the only notification that the execution has been carried out was the erection of a black flag at the tower next to the prison, known as Clifford's Tower. The governor Captain Twyford and the High Sheriff was known to be sympathetic to the press attending the hangings, although the Visiting Justices were very much against it. It was hoped that the governor might allow three newspaper reporters as representatives of the press to be present. Marwood the hangman arrived at York on Monday evening, following another execution he had carried out at Aylesbury. Even though the time was now getting shorter, local reporters felt that the demeanour of the condemned man indicated that he had accepted his fate. This led them to believe that he would probably make a last minute confession. They reported that:

'Whilst apparently most penitent, there is a good deal of dogged determination about his character, and behind this he shelters himself. But this is not at all unusual in the case of condemned criminals who, for some reason which is not clear, refrain from confessing till almost within sight of the gallows'.

It seems that the chaplain spent much of Monday 10 May with the prisoner to prepare him for death, and he rejoined him the next morning, soon after 6 am in his cell. Precisely at 7.45 am that morning the bell began to toll from the nearby St Mary's Church. At the sound many people began to gather around St Georges field opposite, where a good view of the prison walls could be seen. Even at that early hour Marwood had spent some time working on the gallows to ensure that everything went off smoothly. At 7.50 am the Under Sheriff and other officials arrived at the prison, and went straight to the condemned cell along with the governor. There they found Wood standing in the centre of his cell, looking pale but firm. A few moments later Marwood appeared and pinioned the prisoner, who never spoke a word but just uttered a great sigh. At exactly 8 am the procession left the prison led by the governor and deputy governor Mr Triffitt, the chaplain Rev. Baldwin, the two prison surgeons, Mr W C Anderson and Dr Tempest Anderson and the Under Sheriff, William Gray. These were followed by Wood and immediately behind him were two warders who were there to give support to the prisoner if needed. However the prisoner walked with a firm step and made his way to the gallows without showing any fear.

As soon as he stood in position on the trapdoor, Marwood put a rope around his neck, strapped his legs together and placed a white cap over his head. At this point the governor went over to Wood and asked him if he had anything to say, but the prisoner did not respond. The governor took this to mean that he didn't and shouted to the few reporters gathered around the gallows, the word 'No'. Marwood pulled the bolt and the prisoner quickly disappeared from view. Immediately, as the prisoner went through the trapdoor, an official stationed on Clifford's Tower ran up the black flag at half mast and it fluttered in the morning breeze. After hanging for an hour the body of John Henry Wood was cut down and conveyed back into the cell where he had spent his last hours. Then, as was usual, an inquest was held. The jury went to see the body at 11 am and it was reported that the prisoners face appeared calm and placid and his eyelids were closed, suggesting that he had died peacefully. However around his neck the mark of the rope could still be seen. Officials gave evidence that the execution had been carried out according to the law. The coroner in summing up asked the jury:

'Are you all satisfied that the body of the man you have seen this morning was that of the person who was tried and convicted at the last York Assizes? Are you satisfied with the evidence adduced at this inquest, that judgement of death has been duly executed according to the law upon John Henry Wood, who was sentenced to be hanged?'.

The jury replied in the affirmative and gave their opinion that the sentence had been carried out judiciously. After the inquest the body was interred in a piece of ground within the prison walls which had been set aside for that purpose. Wood never made a last confession, however it was later reported that on the night before the execution he had told the chaplain, Rev. Baldwin that 'he knew more about the murder than he intended to make known'. He admitted that he could have told him more, but that he wasn't going to, and stated that although 'he had not been involved in the murder, he did have the dead mans watch'. However he refused to tell the chaplain what he had done with the watch. So died the man accused of being the murderer of John Coe.

The last word has to be left with the Hon. and Rev. Canon Howard, the Vicar of Whiston as well as a Justice of the Peace for the West Riding. He was a very kind man and when he was unsuccessful at visiting Wood in his condemned cell, he didn't want to give up on him. He made a decision which would help the family of his former parishioner, when he informed them that he intended holding a service for Wood at Whiston Parish Church at the exact moment of his execution. It was reported that considering the early hour, there was a good attendance at the Church, where the congregation held a Litany and said silent prayers. Sadly the only member of Wood's family who felt able to attend was his sister-in-law Mrs Charles Greaves, although other relatives stayed at home with drawn blinds across the windows. It had been hoped that Wood might have sent another letter to relatives or friends before his death, but none were reported. Nevertheless for many months afterwards the murder and execution of John Henry Wood was discussed and gossiped about, as if local people and the newspapers were reluctant to let go of the subject. Much of the interest was because, although some thought that the guilty man had paid for his crime on the scaffold, there were many discrepancies which remained unanswered.

Chapter Eleven: Conclusions

From this distance of time it is hard to judge objectively about how or why John Coe was murdered, but from the newspapers reports at the time there were intriguing clues which are simply left hanging. The first clue was the man Charles Staunton who was mentioned by Wood's defence Mr Gane in his speech at the trial. When speaking of the two men's visit to the house of 'Big Liz' he said:

'They left behind in the house a man named Charles Staunton, who did not live there, and on whose whereabouts since, no light has yet been thrown'.

Why mention him at all, if he had nothing to do with the case? No doubt in a brothel there were many other dubious men at the time, so why single him out in a defence speech. Also it has to be questioned why did the man Staunton suddenly decamp, unless he had something to do with the crime? Did he have a grudge against Coe, which might have involved the prostitute who went outside with him, according to Wood's statement to Superintendent Gillett on the evening of the murder? Was Wood given the watch to ensure his silence? This would also answer Woods statement made to both the chaplain and to his parents that he had possession of the watch, but had taken no part in the murder. I have researched diligently for any mention of Staunton in police records or newspaper reports, but have found nothing apart from the single mention in the defence's summing up in the *Sheffield and Rotherham Advertiser* dated Saturday 6 March 1880. I have also looked for any other reports that Coe went outside with a prostitute, but, no doubt with the fear of outraging prudish Victorian sensibilities, no other newspapers stated it. If someone called Staunton did have a grudge against Coe, it could also explain the vicious way in which the body had been so brutally attacked. Modern forensics would label such a murder as a determined 'hate' crime, due to the ferocity of the attack. Even at the time it was recognised that the assault had been 'so hard that the front of Coe's head had literally been smashed in'. (*York Herald* dated 21 Feb 1880)

However my research indicates that that a much more plausible murderer might have been the man named Charles Young who met Wood at the Stag the day after the murder, and who gave evidence as a witness at both the magistrates court and the trial. Young, like Wood was well known to the local police as a thief and a brothel keeper and was also known by alias's of 'Mills' and 'Chitty Mills'. He was certainly running a brothel in October 1877 which involved one of the prostitutes, a girl named Mary Ann Daley who was also a well known thief. Nine months later Young was listed as living at 125 Wellgate, which was possibly close to the actual building, where 'Big Liz' kept her own brothel. Two years later in May 1879 he had been charged with being drunk and disorderly and was sent to the Wakefield House of Correction. It might have been this sentence that he was overheard discussing with Woods in the Stag Inn on 19 February 1880. What is interesting is that previously Mary Ann Daley, then his wife, was arrested in July 1878, charged with stealing a silver watch and gold guard from a man called Charles Ward in Rotherham. The similarities were uncanny in that, like Coe, she had met him at the Pack Horse Inn before taking him to 'a house of ill repute in Old Hill, Wellgate' where he was robbed. Although Daley pleaded not guilty to the theft, she was sent to prison for six months with hard labour. If she had been guilty of the same crime of stealing the watch and cash from John Coe in February 1880, she knew she that this time she would have been given a much longer sentence by the magistrates. The theft of the articles would also answer the cabman Holmes' evidence, when he overheard one of the two men say to the other that 'they would make the beggars pay for it' on the night of the murder. Had Young attacked and killed John Coe to prevent him from reporting Daley for the robbery? It would also explain why the two men left the house suddenly and without warning, once Coe found the articles were missing. Again it is possible that Wood was given the watch to keep silent. However most damning of all for Young was the fact that in September 1880, seven months after the murder, he was charged with assaulting Daley. She ominously told the police that 'he [Young] knew more about the murder of John Coe than he had let on at the time'. However despite being closely questioned, she would say no more.

Wood was well known to associate with other criminals, and yet he had a strong sense of loyalty towards them. We know in the past, it had been reported in local newspapers, that Wood had taken the blame and served a sentence for a crime he did not commit rather than give the police the names of the true criminals. His comments were such that he knew very well who had killed John Coe, which validate his comments to the chaplain and his family, that he had possession of the watch, but was not guilty of the murder. When pushed to confess he told the prison chaplain at York, Rev. Baldwin that he could tell him more, but he preferred to keep his own counsel. Although the probability is that Wood didn't kill Coe - it is almost certain that he knew who did, and therefore went to his death with fortitude whilst still proclaiming his innocence.

The fact that this and many other crimes remained unsolved at the time is not very surprising, as during the Victorian period there was little forensic understanding that we have today. As we have seen, when analyst Dr Alfred Henry Allen was giving evidence at the magistrates court he had no way of knowing if the blood on the hedge stick or Woods clothing was human. Indeed the only way of deciding was to compare it with a sample of his own blood to see if there was any similarities. Having said that, it did not take modern forensic techniques to know that a person who battered in the front of John Coe's head would have to be saturated with that blood, and Woods clothes were not. This fact alone should have entitled Wood to the benefit of 'Reasonable Doubt' and acquittal. Even the timescales of the murder was only supposition and the fact that the crime might have been committed later than the given estimate of midnight by Dr Junius Hardwicke, might have gone towards hiding the actual killer. Firstly Dr Hardwicke arrived about 9.25 am and reported the body as still being warm, yet we have to question how was this possible if, as he stated, the man had been killed and left outside around midnight, in February. At the time great emphasis was put on statements made by medical men over other non professionals. To the point where judges and coroners frequently advised juries to ignore the evidence of witnesses, if it contradicted that of a surgeon. The fact that several of the witnesses, including a police officer, stated they had seen either a movement of the deceased mans leg, or fresh blood pouring from him would substantiate this theory. George Hall saw the body at 7 am and thought he saw the leg move. Joseph Hawksworth, John and George Swallow and Sergeant Morley all saw blood coming from the mans wounds at between 8-9 am, although Hawksworth was unsure by the time he got to the Assizes. Secondly if the Cabman William Holmes stated that at around 11.40 pm both men were seen alive at the High Street. Could they have travelled along Westgate to Canklow Road, gone to the field, taken time to make a bed from straw, before John Coe was viciously attacked, all in 20 minutes according to Dr Hardwicke's conclusions?

Wood told his family before he died that he had not visited Rotherham more than four times in his whole life, and did not know for certain the field in which the body had been found. If Wood had left Coe to make his own way home as he had said in his statement, he would not know the field in which the body was found. Had he indeed left him as he stated on Wellgate? If he had was he aware that Charles Young or the man Staunton, was following Coe and meant him harm? Did they agree to meet up the next day when the silver watch would be handed over to Wood for his silence? Finally, if we decide that Wood is guilty we must question why, when up to that time he only had a history of petty thieving, would he suddenly escalate to a terrible and unprovoked murder? Modern criminologists studying why people commit murder today, see it as a progression from petty acts, to more serious activities before the actual crime of murder is perpetrated. As stated in the trial the two men had been on the best of terms, with Coe buying Wood many drinks on their last journey together. His own father spoke about his sons amiable behaviour, which would hardly incite another to sudden violence. I would suggest that men like Charles Young or the mysterious Staunton would be more capable to commit a deed which would rob a young man of his life. Perhaps the biggest mistake that John Coe made on the night he was killed, was to visit the brothel of the woman known as 'Big Liz'. Was this yet another of the countless crimes caused by someone being 'in the wrong place at the wrong time'. We shall never know.

Other Books By Margaret Drinkall

If you have enjoyed reading this book, then here are some more written by the same author and easily accessible to download onto a kindle device immediately or to buy in book form on Amazon. Some are 19th century crimes committed in Britain generally, whilst other focus on the town of Rotherham itself.

Rotherham Crime Books:

AN ALMANACK OF CRIME IN VICTORIAN ROTHERHAM

This is a grim, though true, snapshot of what life was like in the town of Rotherham during the Victorian era. Whilst many were celebrating the expansionism of the Industrial Revolution and the Empire, most people just lived their lives in the best way they could. Where better to see this than in the court cases of the time. Within these pages read about cases of women arrested wearing men's clothes, concealment of birth, more exploits of 'Rotherham Bob' and a slippery thief who managed to pawn the same wheelbarrow twice.

MORE NINETEENTH CENTURY ROTHERHAM MURDERS

Many of these cases have been drawn from those published in Margaret Drinkall's weekly column in the *Rotherham Advertiser,* but they have been expanded to include much more details. For example there is a case of a young boys killed by a stagecoach that was travelling too fast along Westgate. There is the murder of a farmer at Thrybergh, that remained unsolved to this very day, despite a reward and an allegation made twenty six years later. There is an attempted murder at the canal side in Rotherham where a man tries to kill his wife. Another man tried to kill his wife at the Dusty Miller public house, by shooting at her. But perhaps the most serious attempted murder was that of a man who tried to kill his former landlord and his wife. He had wanted her to elope with him, but she refused and the actual letters they sent each other are reproduced. In addition there is a case of a shoot out on Wellgate at the Cleaver Inn, and other true crimes such as poaching, highway robbery, infanticide as well as a man who claimed to be imitating Jack the Ripper. All these crime took place in the same lanes and street in which modern people of Rotherham walk along today

ROTHERHAMS ROGUES AND VILLAINS

This book has six new cases, which have never been written about before concerning some of the rogues and villains of the town of Rotherham. The cases include:
An sudden and unprovoked attack on an elderly man, by a younger one he befriended in Conisbrough. The two men had formed an unlikely friendship for many years until the sudden, murderous attack which completely came out of the blue. The second case is one which broke a gang of robbers that had been operating in the area around Rawmarsh for many years. The Rotherham police force looked on helplessly as the crimes continued, and which were only broken when four men of the village took the law into their own hands. The third case also holds a mystery. Did a harassed servant girl take her revenge on her controlling mistress by poisoning her, or was she completely innocent pawn? Only you can decide. The fourth case is a massive jewel robbery of which a local rogue, a man called 'King Dick' was strongly suspected. Failure to catch the thieves for this crime, or the many other robberies that remained unsolved in the area, brought the reputation of the Rotherham police force into strong disrepute. The fifth case is a couple who lied and cheated people into supplying them with goods, on the understanding that they would be re-paid. The last case is that of a disaffected solicitors clerk from Wath. When his former employers refused to pay the money that he felt he was owed, he maligned them in placards which were placed in the windows of his house, for all the world to see.

ROTHERHAM CRIMES

This is another book of true crimes in Rotherham which took place in the 19th century. Many of these cases have been published in Margaret Drinkall's weekly column in the *Rotherham Advertiser* but they have been expanded to include more details and the actual statements made by the witnesses and those accused of crimes. The book includes the case called 'Consider Me Dead' about breach of promise case. This expanded version introduces the actual love letters between the couple, plus two vicious ones that the allegedly 'demure Miss Glover' had sent to Mr Straw's ex-girlfriends. There are more swindles uncovered when William and Eliza Fritz came to Rotherham reporting that they had come into money. The tradesmen of the town were eager to supply them with goods and food on the expectation that they would be paid when the couple came into their inheritance. They did not realise they had been duped, until the couple skipped town. There is the mysterious poisoning of a woman called Mrs Bates who was visiting the town from Birmingham. When she died after eating some sausages, the police were not notified and no inquest was held until her husband heard rumours that she had been poisoned. Other case involve a smooth talking clog dancer, the notorious Mrs Barton a brothel house keeper and the strange case of Eli Swift

ROTHERHAM CRIMES 2

This is a new selection of expanded reports, that were previously published in the Rotherham Advertiser. These are events that really happened here in Rotherham, over a hundred years ago. They range from a belief in witchcraft, murder and suicide at Conisbrough, a boy who killed a headmasters pet jackdaw, to three tragic concealment of birth cases. Attempted murders, committed without any logic or reason. There is also the case of a gang of 22 boys, brought before the magistrates for thieving. On their way, they were marched through Rotherham's streets like heroes.

MISCREANTS AND MURDERERS IN VICTORIAN ROTHERHAM

Who would have thought that on the bridge which still holds an ancient chapel, a man was murdered for no reason at all. By now, most people are aware of the problems facing women giving birth to an illegitimate child in Victorian society. But who would believe that a respectable farmer could impregnate his housekeeper and yet deny all knowledge of it, despite her statement to the contrary. There is a compelling account of an embezzlement at Bentley's Brewery, and the way in which the thief was detected, using common sense police methods, long before the development of the forensic science we have today. The book also has an account of a robbery at an isolated toll bar whose keeper kept a loaded pistol, cocked and ready to fire on the mantelpiece. A neighbours quarrel, which illustrates the low lifestyle of people living in the rabbit warren of yards off Westgate. But the most terrible of all these is the case of the brutal neglect of a father towards his daughter, who in his eyes, brought the ultimate shame to his door.

MYSTERY MURDER AT BOLTON-UPON-DEARNE

On 5 December 1856 two elderly people were murdered in their home, bludgeoned to death during an apparent robbery. The wounds inflicted on them were so severe, that two doctors and the coroner stated that over many years of practice, they had never seen such violence before. Although the case was never solved at the time, new research has brought a possible killer to light. Was he the man who took the lives of these eminently respectable people? With the probable criminal, both victim's families and everyone else safely in their graves, the only person left to judge, is you.

ROCHE ABBEY MURDERS

This is the story of two deaths years apart, which was linked by a man's silver watch. By coincidence, both men were related and both were returning home to the village of Stone near Roche Abbey. Neither made it. In the first case a man was hung for the crime, although many people believed that he was innocent. Twenty three years later his nephew disappeared under strange circumstances, leaving the watch he had inherited, behind.

National Crime Books:

MESSENGERS OF DEATH

It was easy to kill someone in the 19th century, much easier than it is today...

Access to arsenic could be gained for pennies and it's effects mimicked such diseases as cholera, dysentery and typhoid, all of which, at the time, were common illnesses. Other killers, such as laudanum, sulphuric acid and a rare poison called colchicum were used by the women in this book. Research proves that it was easier to kill someone by poison in rural areas than in big towns and cities. In most cases, the murder was only brought to the attention of the authorities by gossip and rumour mongering. One expert suggested that there were many hundreds of poisoning cases that remained undetected. It was said that women were more amenable to poisoning as it was a non physical type of execution. They also had less chance of detection, by travelling around the country, getting married and/or changing their name. The insidious ways in which these poisons were used, called for such women to be nicknamed 'Messengers of Death'.

Using previously unexplored cases, Margaret Drinkall reveals how women poisoners in the nineteenth century created such a culture of poisoning, that it seriously alarmed the government and the legal authorities of the time. Some women believed that spells and the power of witchcraft would protect them from the gallows. One woman offered her services as a professional poisoner, to other wives wishing to escape their husbands. Many others enjoyed the benefits of murder after insuring their relatives in burial clubs, *without the knowledge or consent* of those who were poisoned. Women in the village of Wix near Harwich used mass poisonings to rid themselves of encumbrances. As a result, local coroners were forced to order many exhumations. This then is the story of some of those 'Messengers Of Death'...

THE OTHER WHITECHAPEL MURDER

This book deals with the true murder of Harriet Lane in 1874. She was the mistress of a middle class business man called Henry Wainwright and she disappeared on 11 September 1874. Exactly a year later to the very day, Henry asked a former employee to help him remove two parcels from his business address at 215 Whitechapel Road. The man Stokes agreed but was curious about the contents and when his former employer went for a cab he peered inside and to his horror found the chopped up remains of a woman. Following the cab Stokes managed to attract the attention of two constables and Henry was arrested with the remains. Shortly afterwards his brother was also arrested and charged with being an accomplice to the murder. This case has all the components of a typical Victorian murder, the body being transported in a cab and the body being covered in chloride of lime which was thought to destroy the remains, but in fact worked as a preservative. Using the newspapers of the period and the reports of inquests, magistrates court enquiries and the trial itself, the tale unfolds revealing many twists and turns. But what caused a frisson in the minds of the newspaper reading public was that Henry had so nearly got away with it. For a whole year the body had remained hidden and if Henry had sent Stokes for a cab instead of getting it himself, he would never have been convicted.

WOMEN ON THE GALLOWS

These are some of the cases of women who died at the end of an executioners rope for varied crimes from infanticide, murder of a grandchild and an uncle, to a woman charged with being a resurrectionist a few years after the exploits of Burke and Hare. Included are an horrific tale of a woman who took children from a workhouse and starved and beat them until some of them died. There is the case of a hard hearted stepmother who murdered her own children and her stepchildren because they were 'in the way'. Catherine Foster was so beautiful that she was called the Belle of Acton, but that didn't stop her from murdering her husband, because she never loved him and didn't want to be married. A young girl hanged for infanticide who tried to appeal to the other women lodging with her for mercy. None was shown to her and she was arrested and sentenced. All these women all ended up being hung and sometimes even these judicial deaths themselves were so horrific, that calls for the end of capital punishment was heard in Britain. Legal brains even discussed alternatives methods of execution which would hopefully be less traumatic.

ANGEL MAKERS: HOW THE VICTORIANS ENCOURAGED BABY FARMING

Almost everyone knows the name of Amelia Dyer the notorious baby farmer who was hanged in 1896. She is thought to have dispatched as many as 400 children in her career, but she was not on her own. At a time when infanticide was rife there were many more of these women operating in Britain, and the police were powerless to stop them. Only when a Society was formed which made child protection its bedrock were the activities of these woman brought to an end. It has often been suggested that in their time these women murdered thousands of innocent babies. Not for nothing were they known as Angel Makers. These are the stories of just some of them.

ARMLEY GOAL: LIFE AND DEATH IN A VICTORIAN PRISON

When Armley Gaol was built in 1847 it was intended to be one of the most modern and progressive prisons of its kind. Yet within its walls men, women and children as young as eight were kept in virtual solitary confinement for their entire sentences. Inmates were frequently given pointless hard labour punishments, such as turning the crank, and hours spent on the treadmill.

But the worst part was those prisoners found guilty of violent assaults and murder who were subject to harsh floggings, or worse still execution. Within its walls prison officers dealt with recalcitrant prisoners and inmate violence. Prison surgeons had to deal with the reality of disease and poverty, often from inmates just arriving. The prison chaplains did their best for those in their care but it is no wonder many took the chance to escape or commit suicide rather than serve out their sentences, within its walls.

Reading this account of Life and Death in Armley Gaol, will highlight some of the grisly details of prison life. In the end you will be thankful you are just visiting.

Printed in Great Britain
by Amazon